T0323608

Cambridge Elements

Elements in the Problems of God
edited by
Michael L. Peterson
Asbury Theological Seminary

THE PROBLEM OF GOD IN THOMAS REID

James Foster
University of Sioux Falls

CAMBRIDGE
UNIVERSITY PRESS

Shaftesbury Road, Cambridge CB2 8EA, United Kingdom

One Liberty Plaza, 20th Floor, New York, NY 10006, USA

477 Williamstown Road, Port Melbourne, VIC 3207, Australia

314–321, 3rd Floor, Plot 3, Splendor Forum, Jasola District Centre, New Delhi – 110025, India

103 Penang Road, #05–06/07, Visioncrest Commercial, Singapore 238467

Cambridge University Press is part of Cambridge University Press & Assessment, a department of the University of Cambridge.

We share the University's mission to contribute to society through the pursuit of education, learning and research at the highest international levels of excellence.

www.cambridge.org
Information on this title: www.cambridge.org/9781009539036

DOI: 10.1017/9781009270564

© James Foster 2025

This publication is in copyright. Subject to statutory exception and to the provisions of relevant collective licensing agreements, no reproduction of any part may take place without the written permission of Cambridge University Press & Assessment.

When citing this work, please include a reference to the DOI 10.1017/9781009270564

First published 2025

A catalogue record for this publication is available from the British Library

ISBN 978-1-009-53903-6 Hardback
ISBN 978-1-009-27059-5 Paperback
ISSN 2754-8724 (online)
ISSN 2754-8716 (print)

Cambridge University Press & Assessment has no responsibility for the persistence or accuracy of URLs for external or third-party internet websites referred to in this publication and does not guarantee that any content on such websites is, or will remain, accurate or appropriate.

The Problem of God in Thomas Reid

Elements in the Problems of God

DOI: 10.1017/9781009270564
First published online: January 2025

James Foster
University of Sioux Falls

Author for correspondence: James Foster, james.foster@usiouxfalls.edu

Abstract: Thomas Reid was a theist and a philosopher; yet the exact relationship between philosophy and theology in his works is unclear and disputed. The aim of this Element is to clarify this relationship along three lines by exploring the status, function, and detachability of theism with respect to Reid's philosophy. Regarding the first, the author argues that belief in the existence of God is, for Reid, a non-inferential first principle. Regarding the second, the author argues that theism plays at least six different roles in Reid's philosophy. And, regarding the third, the author argues that, despite this, theism is largely detachable from Reid's concept of human rationality and philosophy. What emerges is a picture of the relationship between philosophy and theology in which both inquiries are motivated by natural human curiosity, and both are founded on principles of common sense.

Keywords: Thomas Reid, natural theology, epistemology, design arguments, common sense

© James Foster 2025

ISBNs: 9781009539036 (HB), 9781009270595 (PB), 9781009270564 (OC)
ISSNs: 2754-8724 (online), 2754-8716 (print)

Contents

1 Reid as a Theist and a Philosopher

That Thomas Reid (1710–1796) was a theist and a philosopher is indisputable. In all his writings, both published and unpublished, Reid makes constant reference to God in phrases like "the divine Architect," "the Author of our being," and "the Supreme Governor" (Reid 1995: 207; Reid 2002a: 69; Reid 2010: 226). It is also clear that Reid's philosophy and theology were related. According to student notes on his natural theology lectures, Reid claimed that reason and revelation "are great lights given to us by the father of light and we ought not to put out the one in order to use the other" (Baird in Foster 2017: 29). But what exactly is relationship between philosophy and theology, according to Reid?

The aim of this small Element is to clarify this relationship along three lines. As Reid is famous – or infamous – for his doctrine of common sense, the first question to ask regarding Reid's understanding of the relationship between philosophy and religion concerns the nature of theistic belief. Specifically, is the existence of God a first principle for Reid, is it the conclusion of a rational argument, or is it something one must take on faith without the aid of reason? Following Todd Buras, I will call this the "status question" (Buras 2021: 261). The second question regards the role of religion in Reid's philosophy. Some scholars believe that the existence of God is a bedrock principle of Reid's epistemology, others believe it plays no philosophical function whatsoever, and still others believe the answer lies somewhere between. What I call the "function question" is therefore contested. Finally, the third question follows from the second and asks whether or not Reid thought that belief in the existence of God was necessary for rationality. Although my formulation of this question differs from his, again following Buras, I will call this the "detachability question" (Buras 2021: 261).

To answer these three questions, we will proceed in four parts. This first section is preparatory and lays a foundation for our discussion by giving an overview of relevant portions of Reid's religion and philosophy. In it, we discuss Reid's (1) religious beliefs, (2) understanding of philosophy, and (3) epistemology. The second section addresses the status question. In this section, I will argue that, for Reid, belief in the existence of God is most accurately understood as a non-inferential first principle. The third section then addresses the function question with respect to Reid's epistemology and his account of human of agency. The answer to this question, I believe, is manifold, with Reid describing at least six ways in which theistic belief buttresses human rationality and motivates us to act. Finally, the last section addresses the detachability question. Here I will argue that although Reid thinks belief in the existence of God is a non-inferentially justified first principle, he does not hold that belief in the existence of God is required to be a rational human being. However, since he believes that natural theology, no less than natural science, is founded on first principles, failure to believe in the existence of God leads to a severely diminished view of the universe.

Before turning to Reid, however, I would like to make two notes. The first concerns terminological clarification. It is not unusual in academic literature to distinguish between the terms "religion" and "theology." Yet I have not done so here. When I use the words "religion," "theology," and similar cognates, I mean to refer broadly to discourse about God and issues relating to God. This equivocal use seems to be in line with Reid's own. One distinction I have retained, because we find it in Reid, is the distinction between "natural" and "revealed" theology. Natural theology, in this context, means what is or can be known about God through reason. Revealed theology, by contrast, means what is or can be known about God through revelation.

Second, I would also like to note that, in this Element, I will leave unaddressed several interesting facets of Reid's theology, including his partial answer to the problem of evil, his attempt to discern the nature and attributes of God through natural theology, and his argument for the existence of the immaterial soul.[1] These are worthy topics of discussion, but for the sake of focus and clarity, I pass by them here.

1.1 Reid's Moderate Religion

Broadly, Reid's revealed theology may be described as moderate and orthodox. In Reid's time, the designation "moderate" signaled allegiance to one of the two principal factions within the Church of Scotland. The first were the "Moderate Literati." Members of this faction accepted traditional Christian doctrines like the incarnation and resurrection but were not staunch Calvinists. They also supported the right of the nobility to appoint pastors to lead congregations on their land, and believed the cultivation of educated tastes to be fully consonant with, and indeed helpful in the pursuit of, a faithful Christian life. Against this moderate party stood the "evangelical" or "popular" party, who accused the Moderates of both heresy, for their apparent divergence from the Westminster Confession and their support of patronage, and of moral backsliding, on account of their interest in polite manners and support of the theater.[2] Although Reid was not active enough in church politics to be counted as a full member of the Moderate Party, his sympathies were clearly with them. Reid criticizes the Calvinists for depreciating

---

[1] See Reid (2010: 259–269), Baird in Foster (2017: 81–123), and Reid (2002a: 617–631).

[2] For a thorough account of the complex theological and philosophical disagreements between and among the moderate and evangelical parties, see especially Sher (2015) and Ahnert (2014).

human nature so thoroughly that they "put out the light of nature and reason in order to exalt revelation" and "cut the sinews of action and obligation" (Reid 2010: 268). He personally benefitted from and supported the patronage system in Scotland's churches and universities. He believed in the salutary moral effects of education and culture, and he supported the theater. Yet, despite the insinuation of some anti-moderates that their opponents were heretics, his theology appears to be both sincere and broadly orthodox.

Indeed, the most remarkable thing about Reid's revealed theology is how unremarkable it is. Reid was a parish minister in the Church of Scotland for fourteen years before becoming a professional academic and appears to have carried out his duties faithfully and with little controversy despite the fraught theological climate of his day.[3] Indeed, in church matters, Reid seems to have been intentionally nonsectarian. It is true that, in an unpublished response to Joseph Priestly, Reid rejects the Roman Catholic doctrine of transubstantiation on the grounds of its absurdity – an expected position for a Presbyterian in Reid's time (Reid 1995: 195). But in a later letter, he also seeks common accord with an unnamed Catholic correspondent, writing that he hopes one day the "pure wine of Rome and Geneva may mix, leaving the dregs behind" (Reid 2002b: 223). A statement such as this could indicate a nonsectarianism so broad as to be unorthodox, an impression that is strengthened by the fact that Reid did not retain his lecture notes from his course on natural theology and, although he occasionally quotes scripture, he rarely discusses specific Christian doctrines in his published works. Yet contemporary sources, such as the student notes from his lectures on natural theology at Glasgow, and testimonies from friends and acquaintances, paint the picture of a typically moderate and pious Presbyterian professor.

For instance, according to the anonymous "Sketch of the Character" of Reid, which appeared in the Glasgow Courier following his death in 1796, Reid "venerated *Religion*; not the noisy contentious systems which lead men to hate and persecute each other, but the subline principle which regulates the conduct by controuling the selfish, and animating the benevolent affections" (Reid 2021: 181, emphasis in original). Further, although both this quotation and Reid's published philosophy emphasize the virtuous effects of religion, we have several pieces of evidence which indicate that Reid's religion was more than moral. One is that, in a late manuscript, Reid writes approvingly of the Christian hope of resurrection (see Reid 1995: 124). And another comes to us from the pen of the evangelical minister James Mackinlay. In his memoirs,

---

[3] For more on Reid's ministry, see Foster (2017: 4–5) and Fraser (1898: 30–42), although the best account will undoubtedly be found in Wood's forthcoming *The Life of Thomas Reid*.

Mackinlay reports that when Reid preached in university chapel at Glasgow, "he seemed to pour out his whole soul and while speaking of the dying love of Christ, tears were observed running down his cheeks, showing the intensity of his inward emotion" (Mackinlay 1843: 14, printed in Reid 2021: 340).[4] Thus, Reid's most careful biographer, Paul Wood, is most likely correct when he describes Reid as someone who was "unsympathetic to the doctrinaire Calvinist orthodoxy of the high flyers within the Kirk" and who avoided "disputes over arcane matters of theology" while subscribing to "a moderate Calvinism which stressed the moral teachings of Christ and which recognized the complimentary provinces of reason and revelation" (Wood "Introduction": lxxiv, in Reid 2021).

An examination of Reid's revealed theology is, therefore, of little interest here. He appears to have had no intention to deviate from a broad Christian orthodoxy, to have applied the same broad standard of orthodoxy to others, and to have avoided theological debates. By contrast, his view that the existence of God can be known through reason and his frequent invocations of God in his published and unpublished works make his natural theology a topic of considerable interest for readers of his philosophy, especially since the status, role, and detachability of theism within it is contested.

1.2 Reid's Baconian Philosophy

While Reid avoided conflict regarding revealed religion, his philosophy was intentionally polemic. Reid's combative philosophical approach was a product of his staunch Baconianism, a theme that runs through all his works. According to Reid, "[t]he rules of inductive reasoning, or of a just interpretation of nature, as well as the fallacies by which we are apt to misinterpret her language have been, with wonderful sagacity, delineated by the great genius of Lord Bacon: so that his *Novum organum* may justly be called *a grammar of the language of Nature*" (Reid 2003: 200, emphasis in the original). This quotation is helpful for understanding Reid's philosophy for two reasons. First, it shows us the high regard Reid had for Francis Bacon's *New Organon*. And second it presents us with three aspects of Bacon's philosophical project that influenced Reid's philosophy: the importance of induction, Bacon's account of the common ways in which philosophers go wrong, and Bacon's understanding of the scope of natural philosophy. There is much that could be said about Reid's appropriation of Bacon.[5] But by taking a quick look at each of these three aspects, we may acquire a good idea of Reid's philosophical method.

---

[4] Although, cf. Reid's comments on the "Eloquence of the Pulpit" in Reid (2004: 240–250), see also my editor's introduction in Foster (2017).

[5] For more on this subject, see especially Davenport (1987), Callergård (2010), Wood's introduction in Reid (2017), and the first chapter in Foster (2024).

Today, both the "hard" and "soft" sciences progress through a broadly Baconian process of experiment and observation. Trials are run, samples are collected, data is analyzed, and, finally, a theory is proposed, which "fits" the data. That theory is then tried again and again against more experiments and more observations until it is either confirmed by experience or proven false by failing to predict observed phenomena. With some caveats, this methodology is relatively uncontroversial today. In Reid's day, however, the use of induction in philosophy – which at that time included most of the topics we now think of as "science" – was viewed with some suspicion. A philosophical preference for deduction over induction – that is, for truth-preserving inferences from absolutely true principles over the creative act of providing the best explanation for available data – is, of course, ancient. It goes back at least to Plato. But, according to Reid, the suspicion of induction and the preference for syllogistic reasoning was given new life in the work of Descartes who, in the *Meditations*, famously refused to believe anything except those principles that could be proven necessarily true and what could be logically deduced from them (see Reid 2002a: 115, 138). Thus the first aspect of Reid's Baconianism is his rejection of the Cartesian preference for deduction, and professed loyalty to the process of experiment, observation, and induction outlined in the *New Organon*.

The second aspect of Baconianism that we find throughout Reid's philosophy is Bacon's account of how philosophy goes wrong. In the *Essays on the Intellectual Powers of Man*, Reid adopts Bacon's account of common intellectual tendencies that lead to unfounded "anticipations," as opposed to an evidence-supported "interpretation," of nature (Bacon 2002: 38). Bacon calls these misleading tendencies *idola* or idols of the mind and provides a fourfold taxonomy (Bacon 2002: 40–56). Here, however, we may briefly note that they include what Reid, following Isaac Newton, calls "hypothesis," by which he means taking an unsupported proposition as true, instead of properly testing it by means of experiment and observation (Newton 2016: 589; Reid 2002a: 52). This type of error is especially important to Reid because he believes that it is connected to the common philosophical preference for deduction. As Reid sees it, the central problem with the philosophy of his day is that too many have followed Descartes in doubting the truth of everything except for a few, thinly supported hypotheses that they treat as foundational principles, and from which they build elaborate but ultimately false philosophical systems by means of logical deduction. Or as Reid puts it in the *Inquiry into the Human Mind on the Principles of Common Sense*:

> It is genius, and not the want of it, that adulterates philosophy, and fills it with error and false theory. A creative imagination disdains the mean offices of

> digging for a foundation, of removing the rubbish, and carrying materials:
> leaving these servile employments to the drudges in science, it plans a design,
> and raises a fabric. Invention supplies materials where they are wanting, and
> fancy adds colouring and every befitting ornament. The work pleases the eye,
> and wants nothing but solidity and a good foundation. (Reid 2003: 15)

This quotation indicates why, in all his major philosophical projects, Reid attempts to refute the philosophical theory that he variously called the "way of ideas," "theory of ideas," or "ideal theory." Reid's antagonism was spurred both by the popularity of this theory in his time and by his reading of Hume's *Treatise*, which begins with the following declaration:

> All the perceptions of the human mind resolve themselves into two distinct
> kinds, which I shall call IMPRESSIONS and IDEAS. The difference betwixt
> these consists in the degrees of force and liveliness, with which they strike
> upon the mind, and make their way into our thought and consciousness.
> Those perceptions, which enter with most force and violence, we may
> name *impressions*; and under this name I comprehend all our sensations,
> passions and emotions, as they make their first appearance in the soul. By
> ideas I mean the faint *images* of these in thinking and reasoning .... (Hume
> 1978: 1, emphasis in the original)

According to Reid, Hume treats the existence of impressions and ideas as an axiom of his philosophical project because he is part of a tradition in modern philosophy running from Pythagoras and Plato to Descartes, Malebranche, Locke, and Berkeley, which adopts the hypothesis that the existence of things in the mind is certain, while belief in the existence of things in the world requires justification (see Reid 2002a: 104–200). For Reid, Hume is the most important philosopher in this tradition because he shows decisively that, if one starts from the central hypothesis of the way of ideas and proceeds by deduction, the inevitable conclusion is skepticism (see Reid 2002a: 448).

Hume's argument for this skepticism is straightforward. If all we perceive are impressions and their attendant ideas, then we have no way to check their correspondence to anything outside ourselves. Indeed, even our sense of self is suspect because it is generated by an impression of selfhood. Reid credits Hume's bravery in following the way of ideas to its logical conclusion. But rather than accept Hume's skepticism, Reid believes the unlikelihood of this conclusion is cause to think again.

And in thinking again, Reid advances several arguments against the way of ideas and the skepticism that he believes Hume has inevitably drawn from it. One of these is that the ideal theory does not actually provide an explanation of perception, since the ideas and impressions it posits are as, or more, mysterious as the act of perception itself. Another is the argument that the ideal theory errs when it asserts that our sensations resemble the thing signified by them. Yet Reid's chief argument against the way of ideas is that there is little to no evidence for the existence of the mental entities – the "impressions" and "ideas" – which form the basis of the ideal theory, while there is practically insurmountable evidence that our external perceptions are reliable.[6] Reid comically illustrates his point in the *Inquiry* writing, "I resolve not to believe my senses. I break my nose against a post that comes in my way; I step into a dirty kennel; and, after twenty such wise and rational actions, I am taken up and clapt in a madhouse" (Reid 2003: 170). There is, in other words, a hefty burden of proof that the way of ideas has not met, on account of it leading to conclusions that are imprudent at best and practically impossible at worst.

The third aspect of Bacon's methodology that we find in Reid regards natural philosophy's extent or remit. Following Bacon, Reid holds that the point of natural philosophy is to catalogue the regularities of nature and to codify them according to universal rules, and not to speculate about the active causes or agents behind them. As Todd Buras and Rebecca Copenhaver put it, Reid, "like Bacon and Newton," is "searching not for causes but for laws" (Copenhaver and Buras 2015: 2). There are two points worth making about this description of Reid's philosophical aims. The first is that in modern philosophical parlance, we would say that Reid's Baconian philosophy excludes the discussion of both efficient and final causes. According to Reid, there is no place in the study of the natural world for the discussion of active agents or their goals (see Reid 2002b: 139–147). The second is that the inclusion of Newton in the previous quotation is not beside the point. According to Reid, Newton was not only the most successful Baconian natural philosopher, his *regulae philosophandi* or "rules for philosophy" were a distillation of Bacon's method such that "he who philosophizes by other rules, either concerning the material system, or concerning the mind, mistakes his aim" (Newton 2016: 440–442; Reid 2003: 12).

This observation is relevant to any discussion of philosophy and religion in Reid because it excludes the explanatory use of God in the study of nature. By contrast, as he writes in an unpublished response to Joseph Priestley: "There are many important branches of human knowledge, to which Sir Isaac Newton's rules of Philosophizing have no relation, and to which they can with no propriety be applied. Such are Morals, Jurisprudence, Natural Theology, and the abstract Sciences of Mathematics and Metaphysics; because in none of those Sciences do we investigate the physical laws of Nature" (Reid 1995: 186).

These topics are inappropriate areas for Baconian investigation on account of two, often overlapping, reasons. The first is that some of these topics have to do

---

[6] See especially Wolterstorff (2001: 45–95).

with voluntary action. Thus, Reid clarifies that we cannot use Baconian science to study the "voluntary actions of men" because they "can in no case be called natural phenomena, or be considered as regulated by the physical laws of Nature" (Reid 1995: 185). Second, some of these topics – including morals, mathematics, and metaphysics – have to do with necessary truths, for which inductive proof is insufficient.[7] Natural theology, according to Reid, falls afoul of both conditions because it deals with the actions of a voluntary and necessary agent: God.

By making these exclusions, Reid clarifies his Baconian criticism of his fellow philosophers. Reid does not fault the ancients, Descartes, or his followers for using deduction from necessarily true first principles *tout court*. Rather, he faults them for using logical deduction inappropriately, with respect to matters that are contingent. Even with this clarification in mind, however, the earlier quotation may seem odd to those familiar with Reid's published works. For one thing, it seems to put Reid at odds with Newton, who writes that "to treat God from phenomena is certainly part of natural philosophy" (Newton 2016: 589). And, for another, it raises an important question: If Reid does not think that natural theology is part of the study of the natural world, why would he discuss topics in natural theology and continually mention God throughout his philosophical works?

We will not reach a full answer to this question until the end of Section 4. However, we may begin to answer it by noting what Reid says concerning the appropriateness of studying the human mind using Baconian methods:

> The constitution of the human mind, and all that necessarily flows from its constitution ... may justly be considered as part of the great volume of Nature. Being, therefore, the work of Nature, its powers and faculties, their extent and limits, their growth and decline, and their connection with the state of the body may, not improperly, be called phaenomena of Nature. And as far as these phaenomena can, by just induction, be reduced to general laws, such laws may properly be called laws of Nature. (Reid 1995: 185)

In other words, although we can neither predict the actions of voluntary agents nor prove necessary truths by means of observation, experiment, and induction, insofar as a given inquiry interacts with entities regulated by the contingent laws of nature – or "from phenomena," as Newton puts it – we may have occasion to include them in our philosophical investigations. This explains why, for instance, Reid spends considerable time discussing duty in his *Essays on the Active Powers of Man* even though moral philosophy concerns both voluntary

---

[7] Reid nowhere defines metaphysics but, following Bacon, seems to have understood it to mean something like "conceptual analysis" (see Bacon 2002: 109; Reid 2002a: 495; Reid 2002b: 127–128, 157).

agents and necessary truths. Although the actions of agents are not governed by invariable physical laws, and although induction is insufficient to justify (for Reid) necessary moral truths, an examination of the natural faculties by which we make and act upon moral judgments is within the purview of natural philosophy. By extension, then, we may also partially explain why we find discussions of natural theology among Reid's explicitly Baconian philosophical works. Natural philosophy interacts with natural theology when it discusses the capacities of the human mind that allow us to rationally acknowledge the existence and character of God.

1.3 Reid's "Common Sense" Epistemology

The influence of Bacon's methodology is closely linked with Reid's appeals to "common sense." This term, however, can be misleading, as Reid himself understood. By way of explanation, the first thing to say is that, by "common sense," Reid does not mean general opinion, or the homespun wisdom of the common person. Rather, what Reid means by "common sense" is the capacity of all rational beings to make accurate judgments based on non-inferential evidence. Somewhat unhelpfully, Reid uses the catch-all term "self-evidence" for this non-inferential evidence; and while he is not entirely clear about the boundaries of this category, he includes within it the evidence of logical necessity, definition, and sensation (see Reid 2002a: 229, 455–456). Essentially, Reid believes that human beings are just the type of beings who have the natural disposition to make rational judgments when certain types of non-inferential evidence are put before them. Reid's epistemology is therefore externalist in this sense: He does not believe that all propositions must be justified by further propositions, but that some propositions are justified by (self-)evidence.

Reid calls the true propositions that are affirmed through judgments about non-inferential evidence "first principles" and "principles of common sense" (Reid 2002a: 452). And these, he tells us, come in two varieties: necessary and contingent. Contingent first principles "are probable, in various degrees" corresponding to the strength of their evidence (Reid 2002a: 455). As examples of such contingent principles Reid lists, among others, "the thoughts of which I am conscious are the thoughts of a being which I call *myself*, my *mind*, my *person*," "[w]e have some degree of power over our actions, and the determinations of our will," and "[t]he natural faculties, by which we distinguish truth from error, are not fallacious" (Reid 2002a: 472, 478, 480, emphasis in the original). These are principles that Reid believes we may treat as certain based on the evidence we have for them and our natural propensity to assent to them. But they are contingent because it is theoretically possible that they are false. Necessary truths, on the other hand, are those whose "contrary is impossible" (Reid 2002a: 456).

Reid's epistemology is, therefore, foundationalist. But, as John Greco puts it, his foundationalism is both "moderate and broad" (Greco 2004: 148). Reid's foundationalism is moderate because our faculties of judgment, though reliable, are fallible. And it is broad because he believes that there are a great many foundational principles. Reid's epistemology is therefore much more flexible and much less brittle than the name "foundationalism" often implies. One can be wrong about first principles in both directions – that a given proposition is or is not one, is or is not true – or even ignorant of certain first principles, and still have a generally accurate understanding of the world, still count as a rational agent.

Naturally, Reid's epistemology prompts many questions, and has generated an extensive scholarly literature.[8] But we now have enough to turn to the three questions that chiefly concern us in this work regarding the relationship between religion and reason in Reid. In the next section, we begin by asking the status question, which seeks to understand whether or not theism is, for Reid, an object of rational assent, and if so, whether or not it is a first principle.

2 The Question of Status in Reid's Epistemology

Within Reid scholarship, there is a debate regarding the status of belief in the existence of God. Traditionally, interpreters have understood Reid to hold that belief in the existence of God is not a first principle. Rather, according to this line of interpretation, theism, for Reid, is a conclusion that must be reasoned to. I call this the "inferential interpretation." Recently, however, this traditional interpretation has been challenged by Buras, who believes that Reid thinks the existence of God is a first principle delivered by our sense of aesthetic taste.[9] This interpretation I call the "non-inferential interpretation."

The purpose of this section is to argue that the non-inferential interpretation is correct. To make this argument, we will first examine Reid's use of a design argument for the existence of God, given in the *Intellectual Powers*. Next, I will argue that Buras is correct that, for Reid, theistic non-inferential judgments are the product of our sense of aesthetic taste. In the last part of this section, however, I will offer a different interpretation than Buras does regarding Reid's use of the syllogistic design argument. According to Buras, Reid offers his syllogistic design argument to "boost" his readers' confidence in the existence of God by

---

[8] See especially Wolterstorff (2001), Van Cleve (2015), and Shrock (2017).
[9] See also Callergård (2010: 118).

showing that it coheres with other first principles. By contrast, I think Reid chiefly appeals to design in defense of theism not by offering arguments, but by offering examples that are intended to trigger common-sense belief, and that the design argument in the *Intellectual Powers* is intended as an illustration, and not as a demonstration of the existence of God.

2.1 Reid's Design Argument for the Existence of God

Although Reid did not retain notes from his lectures on natural theology, given during his teaching career in Glasgow, there are five extant sets of student notes (see Tuggy 2004: 306–307 n). These notes show us that Reid, following tradition, divided the topic of natural theology into three subtopics: the existence of God, the nature and attributes of God, and the works of God (see Baird in Foster 2017: 30). While all of the material recorded in the student notes sheds light on Reid's intellectual project, in this Element, we are most concerned with answering the status, function, and detachability questions. And with respect to these, it is the first division that is most illuminating.

In the student notes from his lectures, Reid is reported to have made at least five different arguments for the existence of God: a cosmological argument, a design argument, an argument from the near-universal belief in divinity and an afterlife, an argument from the apparent contingency of the world, and an argument based on miracles (see Tuggy 2004: 291). Of these, however, Reid devotes the most attention to the design argument in his lectures and reportedly called it "the argument which of all others makes the deepest impression on thinking men" (Baird in Foster 2017: 42). It is also the only argument that receives sustained attention in his published works. Our discussion of the status question will therefore focus on this argument.

The most extensive design arguments we have from Reid appear in two places: In George Baird's lecture notes from Reid's last lectures on natural theology in 1780, and in the *Intellectual Powers*. Interestingly, although they both appeal to apparent marks of design in nature as evidence of the existence of God, they differ in form. In the *Intellectual Powers*, the design argument appears as part of a larger argument regarding necessary first principles, and is given in a compact, syllogistic form.

> The argument from final causes, when reduced to a syllogism, has these two premises: *First*, That design and intelligence in the cause may, with certainty be inferred from marks or signs of it in the effect. This is ... the *major* proposition of the argument. The *second*, which we call the *minor* proposition is, "That there are in fact the clearest marks of design and wisdom in the

works of Nature"; and the conclusion is, that the works of Nature are the effects of a wise and intelligent cause. One must either assent to the conclusion, or deny one or other of the premises. (Reid 2002a: 509–510, emphasis in the original)

In the "Lectures on Natural Theology," by contrast, Reid first spends several lectures giving example after example of apparent design before briefly discussing the same syllogism we find in the *Intellectual Powers*. According to Baird, however, Reid did not fully endorse this syllogistic "argument from *final causes*," declaring that he would "use it without enquiring into the propriety of it" (Baird in Foster 2017: 76, emphasis in the original). Reid's circumspection regarding the classic, syllogistic design argument and the stylistic difference between it and his myriad examples are curious, but neither approach is novel. Rather, both are standard eighteenth- and nineteenth-century tropes, most famously employed by Paley (see Paley 1802: 1–305). Indeed, to some commenters, Reid's syllogistic design argument seems a rather weak species of the genus. While acknowledging that Reid describes many instances of apparent design in nature in the "Lectures on Natural Theology," M. A. Stewart, for example, calls the version given in the *Intellectual Powers* "trite" due to its lack of examples (Stewart 2004: 148). Similarly, Dale Tuggy believes that the argument is flawed due to problems with its major premise.

According to Tuggy, one problem with the major premise of Reid's design argument is that it is equivocal, and may be rendered in two ways:

> Ia. Necessarily, if anything exhibits marks of design then it was caused to exist by at least one intelligent agent.
>
> Ib. Necessarily, if anything exhibits marks of design, we can infer with a high degree of certainty that it was caused to exist by at least one intelligent agent. (Tuggy 2004: 294)

For Tuggy, the problem with Ia is that it is not true. "Some examples of apparent design do come from unintelligent causes; pebbles on some beaches are nicely arranged according to size, yet the arranger was merely the waves" (Tuggy 2004: 295). The problem with the second is that it would make the argument invalid. In response, Tuggy suggests a third version:

> Ic. Necessarily, if anything exhibits marks of design, then it is overwhelmingly probable that it was caused to exist by at least one intelligent agent. (Tuggy 2004: 296)

In sorting through these options, our previous discussion concerning Reid's understanding of the nature and scope of Baconian philosophy is helpful. For one, it helps explain why Reid proceeds by syllogism when, according to

Stewart, "Reid did not believe in syllogisms!" (Stewart 2004: 148).[10] In support of this assertion, Stewart points to Reid's criticism of the use of syllogism by philosophers ancient and modern. But Reid, as we have seen, did not object to any use of truth-preserving logical operations – that is, deduction. What he objected to was the inappropriate use of the syllogistic method in investigations of the contingent regularities of the natural world.

In Reid's argument for the existence of God, however, we are not solely investigating the contingent regularities of the natural world. Rather, according to Reid, we are also discussing necessary truths relating to the existence of a necessary being. This observation not only makes trouble for Stewart's objection to Reid's use of syllogism, but also Ib and Ic. As Tuggy himself notes, not only does Reid present this syllogistic version of the design argument in a chapter on the first principles of necessary truth, the major premise of Reid's design argument also appears in his list of necessary first principles (Reid 2002a: 503; Tuggy 2004: 296 f). Ib and Ic, by contrast, which aspire only to "a high degree of certainty" and "overwhelming probability," aren't necessary truths.

This leaves Ia as the only plausible interpretation of Reid's major premise. It also returns us to Tuggy's objection against it. How could the proposition "if anything exhibits marks of design then it was caused to exist by at least one intelligent agent" be necessarily true? To find the answer, it is first helpful to see that the metaphysical principle invoked in Reid's design argument appears to be closely related to – and perhaps even a specification of – another principle that Reid claims is necessarily true: "That whatever begins to exist, must have a cause which produced it" (Reid 2002a: 497). Reid's language here is, I believe, intentionally parallel to Hume's in the *Treatise*, where Hume claims that the "general maxim in philosophy, that *whatever begins to exist, must have a cause of existence*" is "neither intuitively nor demonstrably certain" (Hume 1978: 78, 79, emphasis in the original).

Hume's argument against the necessary connection between cause and effect emerges from the theory of ideas. According to Hume, there is no impression of "cause." Therefore, we cannot form an idea of cause by copying an impression. Rather, Hume claims, our idea of cause and effect arises by habit from the "constant conjunction" of succeeding impressions, adding that: "[c]ontiguity and succession are not sufficient to make us pronounce any two objects to be cause and effect, unless we perceive, that these two relations are preserved in several instances" (Hume 1978: 87).

---

[10] One is reminded of the old joke, variously attributed to G. K. Chesterton and Mark Twain, among others: When a woman asked whether or not he believed in infant baptism, he replied, "Believe in it, Madam? I've seen it done!"

The implications of Hume's account of our belief in causes are, as Reid recognized, quite general. If we could not assume that every effect had a cause, then Baconian science and Newtonian physics would be chancy at the best and nonsense at worst. Similarly, Hume's theory renders classic arguments for the existence of God invalid. Consider the cosmological argument. If it is not true that every effect has a cause, then the question "why is there something rather than nothing?" may have no answer at all. Things may simply start existing without any prior cause. Reid gestures toward these connections, writing that, if Hume is correct that there is no necessary connection between cause and effect, it "would put an end to all philosophy, to all religion" (Reid 2002a: 497). Yet Reid does not immediately address the implications of Hume's theory for the cosmological argument. Rather, he saves an explicit discussion of natural theology for his discussion of the major premise of his design argument.

It seems likely that Reid delayed discussing the apparently devastating effect of Hume's philosophy on natural theology because he was aware that the metaphysical principle "whatever begins to exist, must have a cause which produced it" and the major premise of the design argument are closely related. Consider, for example, the way Hume uses his account of cause and effect against a design argument in the *Dialogues Concerning Natural Religion*. In Book II of the *Dialogues*, Philo responds to a design argument given by Cleanthes in this way:

> When two *species* of objects have always been observed to be conjoined together, I can *infer*, by custom, the existence of one whenever I *see* the existence of the other: And this I call an argument from experience. But how this argument can have place, where the objects, as in the present case, are single, individual, without parallel, or specific resemblance, may be difficult to explain. (Hume 1998: 51, emphasis in the original)

In other words, Philo uses something like Hume's account of cause – that it arises from the experience of constant conjunction – to argue that, since the universe is a singular effect with which we have nothing to compare, we lack the evidence necessary to speculate about its cause. To have evidence for a divine creator of this universe, we would need to have the experience of multiple universes, all with their own divine creator, from which we could then infer that our universe too was caused by (a) God. Reid, it seems, agrees with Hume that if we acquire our notions of cause and effect from experience, then the design argument does not work. But Reid does not believe that we get our concept of the necessary connection between cause and effect from experience. On the contrary, Reid argues that, although we often come to know that a given effect or type of effect is the product of a given cause or set of causes through experience, the relation between the concepts of "cause" and "effect" is self-evident and necessary (see Reid 2002a: 497–503).

Thus, we find here a reversal of Reid's usual criticism of Hume: that he uses deduction where only induction is appropriate. In this case, it is Hume – who Reid casts as the greatest contemporary proponent of the syllogistic theory of ideas – who believes that we must withhold our consent from these principles until we complete a series of experiments and observations. Reid, on the other hand, believes that the connections between cause and effect and between marks of design and the existence of designers are necessary truths, and that we are warranted in making logical deductions from them. Prima facie, then, it may seem that Reid has tactically abandoned his professed Baconianism. Yet recalling again that Reid thinks Baconianism has no place in the discussion of necessarily true propositions, Reid's complaint here is of a piece with his complaint against the theory of ideas: It uses an inappropriate methodology for the subject at hand. This observation also helps us interpret Reid's major premise, because it tells us how Reid intends some of his necessary first principles be read: as something like tautologies. It is, according to Reid, a necessary and self-evident truth that things that are caused have a cause. The major premise of Reid's design argument should, it seems, also be read in the same way. Things that are designed – as evidenced by their true marks of design – have a designer.

Against this reading, Ryan Nichols and Gideon Yaffe assert that, in the major premise of his design argument, Reid has mixed metaphysical with epistemological concerns. The focus of their complaint is Reid's assertion that "design and intelligence in the cause, may, *with certainty, be inferred* from marks or signs of it in the effect" (Nichols and Yaffe 2023: §8.3; Reid 2002a: 509, emphasis added). We also see this apparent conflation in Tuggy's discussion about this principle: Ib and Ic attempt to honor the epistemological tone of Reid's major premise, while Ia abandons it. Yet, as I see it, this categorical conflation is less significant than it may at first appear. For one thing, Reid clearly calls this first principle "metaphysical" (Reid 2002a: 495). For another, the epistemological slant in Reid's formulation of this first principle can be easily justified, in two ways. First, it is justified by what he says about necessary first principles. They are, as we have seen, principles that "yield conclusions that are certain" (Reid 2002a: 455). And second, it is justified by the fact that he is describing this metaphysical principle in a book about the intellectual powers of the human mind. Would it have been better, and clearer, for Reid to have separated the metaphysical from the epistemological and written (1) that things with actual marks of a design necessarily have a designer and (2) that therefore the existence of such a designer "may, with certainty, be inferred"? For our purposes, yes; for his, perhaps not. But, in any case, context and charity both point to Ia as the appropriate interpretation of this necessary first principle.

Still, by reading the major premise of Reid's design argument in this way, we run into two immediate problems. The first is that this tautological reading may make it seem that Reid's design argument is indeed trite, not in the sense that Stewart proposes, but in the sense of saying very little. Yet we should not, I think, expect much more from necessarily true statements. They are, after all, propositions whose "contrary is impossible." The second problem is more substantial. By accepting Ia as the correct interpretation of Reid's major premise, we have run head-first into another of Tuggy's objections: Ia cannot be true because certain phenomena appear to be designed but do not have a designer.

In thinking about how Reid might respond to this objection, there are two things worth noticing. The first is that Tuggy's evidence against the truth of Ia is question-begging. Tuggy assumes that pebbles on the beach arranged by waves show that you can have evidence of design without a designer, but Reid would disagree. According to Reid, God is the creator of the universe, and governs it according to contingent but universal law-like relations. Thus, for Reid, the sorted pebbles on the beach actually are evidence of a designer, albeit one, in this instance, who works through the medium of natural laws governing waves and pebbles of various weights. The designer, therefore, may not be the direct cause of naturally arranged pebbles; but the design is no less real for indirection.

Second, if we interpret Ia along the lines I suggest, then Tuggy's argument addresses not the major but the minor premise of Reid's design argument: "[t]hat there are in fact the clearest marks of design and wisdom in the works of Nature." This is because – unless one wishes to take Hume's side regarding cause and effect – the marks of actual, real design in an object do necessarily imply the existence of a designer. The question worth asking, as Tuggy does, however, is whether a given phenomenon – like arranged rocks on a beach – counts as a mark of design. If it does not, then the syllogism fails. Conversely, if it does, then the syllogism is true, on account of the necessary truth of its major premise.

Crucially, this observation brings us from the realm of necessity to the realm of contingent truths. For, if the minor premise is true, it is true not necessarily but contingently. As for whether or not the minor premise is true, I leave to the reader to decide. What is important to us here is that these clarifications bear directly on the status question. For, so far, it seems that Reid's design argument is intended to prove the existence of God through logical inference from the necessary first principle that designed things have a designer and the contingent principle that the world shows marks of (actual) design. Does this then mean that Reid thinks belief in the existence of God is inferential?

2.2 The Inferential Interpretation

According to the inferential interpretation, the answer to the aforementioned question is "yes": Reid does not treat the existence of God as a "first" or "common sense" principle; he treats it as the conclusion of a syllogism. As this interpretation stands upon a straightforward reading of Reid's design argument, it is unsurprising that most commentators who deal with Reid and religion adopt its answer to the status question without supplying further justification. In his entry in the *Cambridge Companion to Thomas Reid*, however, Tuggy helpfully provides four reasons to prefer the inferential interpretation.

First, according to Tuggy, although Reid has influenced the "Reformed Epistemologists," who claim that belief in the existence of God is a "basic" belief – something similar to a Reidian first principle – the amount of time Reid spends on his arguments for the existence of God shows that he differs from them regarding the status of theism (Plantinga 1983: 74). For, while the Reformed Epistemologists disdain the making of arguments for God's existence, Reid, it seems, does not. "Thus he has no sympathy for what Plantinga calls the Reformed objection to natural theology" (Plantinga 1983: 63–71; Tuggy 2004: 299).

Second, Tuggy believes the form of Reid's arguments for the existence of God shows that God's existence is something reasoned to. In the design argument we have already examined, for example, Reid sets up a syllogism with a necessary first principle – Ia – and a contingent first principle – "That there are in fact the clearest marks of design and wisdom in the works of Nature" – which treats the existence of God as a conclusion. According to Tuggy, Reid also used Samuel Clarke's cosmological argument during his natural theology lectures in a similar way: by starting with the necessary first principle that everything that exists must have a cause and the contingent first principle that the universe exists, and then using the assumed impossibility of an infinite regress to conclude that there must be a necessary being that creates the contingent universe (Tuggy 2004: 292). In both cases, the existence of God is a conclusion, not a first principle.

Third, according to Tuggy, Reid nowhere posits anything like John Calvin's *sensus divinitatis*, which, like our external senses, would have to be, on Reid's account, a faculty of common sense (Calvin 1960: 46). Rather, according to Tuggy's Reid, we come to believe in the existence of God in the same way that we believe in the existence of other minds: by observing the apparent purposiveness and effects of their actions and judging that they are active beings. As Tuggy acknowledges, this assertion initially appears to cut against the inferential interpretation in two ways. First, Reid believes that the discernment of intelligence in fellow human beings is a non-inferential judgment based on outward signs of their intelligence. Second, Reid draws a direct line between the our judgments about the intelligence of other people and the existence of the creator, writing that "the best reason we can give, to prove that other men are living and intelligent is, that their words and actions indicate like powers of understanding as we are conscious of in ourselves" and that the "very same argument applied to the works of nature, leads us to conclude, that there is an intelligent Author of nature" (Reid 2002a: 483). Yet Tuggy maintains that our judgments about God must still be inferential because they are not "automatic enough to be a first principle" and "belief in God isn't automatically formed; it isn't inevitable given the normal course of human life" (Tuggy 2004: 300; see also Stewart 2004: 147).

Finally, Tuggy writes that belief in the existence of God does not have the hallmarks of a Reidian first principle. According to Reid, first principles typically are necessary for everyday life, appear so early as to be believed without training or reasoning, are universally believed across history and culture, and lead to absurd conclusions when denied (Reid 2002a: 463–467). Granted, Reid does not think that every first principle must have all of these marks. But if the judgment that God exists was non-inferential, wouldn't it have at least one?

There are several objections one could make against Tuggy's case here. One is that Reid only spends significant time making arguments for the existence of God in his lectures on natural theology; lectures that he was obliged to give as professor of moral philosophy in Glasgow, and the notes of which – for reasons unknown – he did not retain. In his published material, by contrast, Reid spends very little time making such arguments, and makes them only as asides. Another possible objection, which Tuggy himself notes, is that Reid's account of testimony may open an avenue for treating belief in the existence of God as a first principle. Included in Reid's list of first principles of contingent truth, Reid writes that there "is a certain regard due to human testimony in matters of fact, and even to human authority in matters of opinion" (Reid 2002a: 487). Naturally, a great many – perhaps most – theists come to believe in the existence of God on the basis of testimony. If beliefs based on testimony are always, for Reid, first principles, then shouldn't belief in the existence of God be a first principle in such cases?

On examination, neither of these objections makes much trouble for the inferential interpretation. Regarding the first, even though Reid does not spend much time on arguments for the existence of God in his published works, he spends enough. Reid clearly thinks that the cosmological argument and design arguments are arguments.

Regarding testimony, the result is the same. While Reid thinks that it is a first principle that human beings treat testimony as a source of evidence, Reid's first principle regarding testimony does not say that beliefs we receive via testimony are first principles on that basis alone. Rather, Reid is clear that testimony deserves only "a certain regard in matters of fact" (Reid 2002a: 487). One could reply that Reid thinks children are born with a natural disposition to believe what they are told. Yet Reid is clear that this disposition is not itself a form of rationality. Rather, the credulity of children is a temporary condition, instilled by (the Author of our) nature to facilitate rapid learning in early age (Reid 2010: 86–87). Once we are intellectually mature, by contrast, testimony – including religious testimony – must be weighed by reason. According to Baird, Reid instructed his natural theology students that it "is by reason that we must judge whether ... revelation be really so; it is by reason that we must judge the meaning of what is revealed; and it is by reason that we must guard against any impious, inconsistent, or absurd interpretations" (Baird in Foster 2017: 30). Testimony, in other words, must often be weighed before it can be rationally accepted. Exceptional cases aside, it does not therefore seem that belief in the existence of God can be a Reidian first principle on the basis of testimony alone.

2.3 Aesthetic Taste and Non-Inferential Belief in the Existence of God

There are, therefore, strong, textually supported reasons for holding the inferential interpretation. Recently, however, Buras has challenged this view. As he sees it, despite initial appearances, Reid holds that belief in the existence of God is a first principle on account of his understanding of aesthetic taste.

Borrowing a division from contemporary philosophers, Reid posits three qualities that are perceived by the faculty of aesthetic taste: novelty, grandeur, and beauty (Reid 2002a: 579). Novelty, for Reid, is the relation of newness between an observer and a thing, and does not concern us here. Grandeur and beauty, on the other hand, are qualities of objects that our faculty of aesthetic taste perceives. In taking this position, Reid is intentionally setting himself against subjectivist accounts of aesthetic taste, which treat these qualities as purely subjective experiences. For instance, according to Hume, beauty "is felt, more properly than perceived" (Hume 1997: 165). For Reid, on the other hand, subjective experience is only part of the story. There is both a mental event or events in the person observing and an objective quality in the grand or beautiful thing perceived.

A full engagement of Reid's complex account of aesthetic taste is beyond the confines of this little Element.[11] But to understand Buras' non-inferential interpretation, we need only know a little bit about Reid's account of both the observer of a grand or beautiful object and the object being observed. Let us start with the former. According to Reid, our reaction to grandeur and beauty has two parts. "*First*," when we perceive (or imagine) objects of grandeur and beauty "they produce a certain … emotion or feeling" (Reid 2002a: 592, emphasis in the original). Specifically, according to Reid, when encountering grandeur, we experience awe; when encountering beauty, we experience pleasure. Second, this "emotion is accompanied with a belief of their having some perfection or excellence belonging to them" (Reid 2002a: 592). The belief that accompanies the emotive response to a grand or beautiful object is, for Reid, a non-inferential judgment, and it comes in two types. The first type is "instinctive." In this type of judgment, we perceive grandeur and beauty "without our being able to say why we call them" grand or beautiful (Reid 2002a: 596). The second type of judgment made by our sense of aesthetic taste is "rational," and in these the "agreeable [or awesome] quality of the object … is distinctly conceived, and may be specified" (Reid 2002a: 598).

These observations concerning the observer of an aesthetically excellent object lead us to the second part of Reid's understanding of grandeur and beauty – the objects themselves – and the qualities that generate emotions and judgments. According to Reid, another twofold distinction is necessary to understand the nature of grandeur and beauty in objects we perceive through our sense of aesthetic taste. They are "original" and "derived" grandeur and beauty. Original grandeur and beauty are, properly, the qualities of minds. For Reid, these excellences are objective. Is it not better, Reid asks us, for a mind to be wise, noble, upright, and clever than for it to be foolish, ignoble, crooked, and stupid (see Reid 2002a: 585)? According to Reid, it is. Therefore, when we perceive original grandeur or beauty, we are making an objective judgment about a mind. Yet since we cannot directly perceive other minds, we must make such judgments about the grandeur or beauty of minds as they are manifested in their acts and artifacts. And this manifestation, according to Reid, is the derived grandeur and beauty that we observe through our sense of aesthetic taste.

---

[11] The trio of articles by Copenhaver (2015), Zuckert (2015), and Jaffro (2015) in Copenhaver and Buras (2015) is an excellent resource.

This description of Reid's account of aesthetic taste is useful to us here because, as Buras notes, "Reid explicitly models the faculty of taste on the external senses, noting that taste is a faculty for the production of immediately justified, non-inferential beliefs" (Buras 2021: 267). That is, just as our sense of sight tells us, non-inferentially, that there is text before us, so our sense of aesthetic taste may tell us, upon hearing Beethoven's ninth, that there is a great mind at work. A perception of original grandeur or beauty, in other words, is a non-inferential judgment about the quality – and *a fortiori* existence – of another mind.

From here, the argument for the non-inferential interpretation is straightforward. When we find works of art grand or beautiful, we may non-inferentially perceive the excellence of their artists' minds. By the same token, then, Reid must hold that when we perceive the grandness of the night sky or the beauty of a desert flower, we may non-inferentially perceive the excellence and existence of God.

Buras' non-inferential interpretation is supported not only by Reid's philosophical account of aesthetic taste, but also by the frequent examples he gives by way of illustration. "When we contemplate the earth, the sea, the planetary system, the universe," Reid writes concerning grandeur, "it requires a stretch of imagination to grasp them in our minds. But they appear truly grand, and merit the highest admiration, when we consider them as the works of God" (Reid 2002a: 586). Similarly, regarding beauty, he tells us that our judgments of derived and original beauty "may be applied with no less justice to the works of Nature" because the "invisible Creator, the Fountain of all perfection, hath stamped upon all his works signatures of his divine wisdom, power, and benignity, which are visible to all men" (Reid 2002a: 595, 603). Thus, as Laurent Jaffro puts it, for Reid "the immediate inference of design is embedded in the perception of beauty" (Jaffro 2015: 170).

2.4 Objections to the Non-Inferential Interpretation

Like the inferential interpretation, Buras' non-inferential interpretation makes good sense of the textual resources we have from Reid and presents a coherent case. To be convincing, however, the non-inferential interpretation must be able to address Tuggy's four reasons, discussed in Section 2.2, for holding that belief in the existence of God is not a first principle for Reid. They were: (1) that Reid places too much emphasis on arguments for the existence of God for it to be a first principle, (2) that the syllogistic structure of his design argument shows the same, (3) that Reid does not posit a *sensus divinitatis*, and (4) that belief in the existence of God does not share any of the hallmarks of a Reidian first principle.

The first and second may be taken together, for Buras recognizes and antici-
pates the argument that Reid's discussion of the traditional proofs of the
existence of God show that he does not hold theism to be a first principle.
This argument against the non-inferential option is strengthened by Reid's
declarations that first principles "need no proof ... do not admit of direct
proof," and that it is "contrary to the nature of first principles to admit of direct
or *apodictical* proof" (Reid 2002a: 39, 463, emphasis in the original). This not
an idle issue for Reid. As he sees it, the attempted "proof" of first principles is
a favorite trick used by skeptics to undermine confidence in human reason. Yet,
as Gregory Poore has pointed out, in his more careful moments, Reid is not so
absolute regarding the unprovability of first principles. Only a few lines down
from the first quotation above, he equivocates, writing that first principles
"seldom admit of direct proof" (Reid 2002a: 39). He also later clarifies that,
although first principles are not the type of principles that are "built solely on
reasoning," we sometimes may be able to "deduce one [first principle] from
another" (Reid 2002a: 482; Reid 2010: 276).

As Poore reads him, Reid's epistemology does not rule out the possibility that
a first principle could be the conclusion of a proof. But why would such a proof
be useful? As Reid is an externalist and a foundationalist, Poore is clear that by
"arguing that Reid's epistemology contains coherentist strands, I do not wish to
suggest that coherence is the primary, let alone the only, source of justification"
(Poore 2015: 223). Yet, coherence still "has positive epistemic value for Reid
and it can boost, though not supplant, the justification of beliefs formed according to his externalist criteria" (Poore 2015: 223). An example of such an appeal
to coherence may be found in Reid's account of the blind Cambridge mathem-
atician Nicholas Saunderson, who was able to understand how solid figures look
in perspective from his sense of touch and understanding of mathematics (Reid
2003: 95–98).[12] For Dr. Saunderson, this proof was the only way that he could
come to the judgment that solid figures are visually perceived in perspective by
those who have the power of sight. For those with sight, for whom belief in the
phenomena of visual perspective is formed on the basis of a non-inferential
judgment, Dr. Saunderson's proof is not necessary. It may, however, still serve
as a bulwark against skeptical arguments against the existence of the external
world based upon the fact that objects appear differently at different angles and
distances (see, e.g., Sextus Empiricus 2000: 11–12). By analogy, then, one may
suppose that Reid's design argument is intended to offer a second way to assent
to theism, which bolsters the non-inferential judgment of our sense of aesthetic
taste.

---

[12] Reid visited Dr. Saunderson during a trip to London in 1736.

As for Tuggy's third objection, Buras has an easy reply. While it is true that Reid does not specify a special faculty that senses the existence of God, according to Buras, the sense of aesthetic taste can function as a kind of *sensus divinitatis* when we perceive the grandeur and beauty of nature. Thus, Reid did not posit the existence of a special sense for non-inferentially detecting the existence of the deity because he did not need one. The sense of aesthetic taste suffices.

Finally, regarding the objection that belief in the existence of God does not have the characteristics of a Reidian first principle, a proponent of the non-inferential interpretation may respond by pointing to the close connection that Reid makes between belief in the intelligence of other people and belief in the existence of God.[13] As we saw when we examined the major proposition of Reid's design argument, Reid not only believes that it is a necessary truth that "design and intelligence in the cause, may, with certainty, be inferred from marks or signs of it in the effect," but argues at length that it is a first principle (Reid 2002a: 503). In fact, in making this case, he specifically argues that this principle is "too universal to be the effect of reasoning" and leads to absurdity if denied (Reid 2002a: 504). Further, there is no evidence that Reid would have accepted Tuggy's claim that judgments about human intelligence based on external signs of human design are different than judgments about divine intelligence because the latter are not "automatic enough." On the contrary, Reid is clear that, just as we believe in the intelligence of other people on account of the outward signs of their intelligence, so belief in God "appears equally strong and obvious" to most people who perceive the grand and beautiful in nature (Reid 2002a: 483).

2.5 The Purpose of Reid's Design Arguments

On account of the relative strength of Buras' arguments, I believe that the non-inferential interpretation makes better sense of what Reid says about belief in the existence of God than the inferential option. However, while I agree with Buras about the status of theism in Reid, I disagree with him regarding Reid's intended use of the syllogistic design argument in the *Intellectual Powers*. Using Poore's terminology, we can say that Buras suggests that Reid uses this argument to make theism a "super-justified" first principle (Poore 2015: 224). As mentioned previously, however, Reid approaches the relationship of apparent marks of design and the existence of God in two different ways: In the *Intellectual Powers*, he presents the syllogistic argument we have just been discussing, but in the "Lectures on Natural Theology," he chiefly gives examples of design in nature. In what follows, I argue that these two types of "argument" are directed to two very different purposes.

---

[13] On this point, see Kroeker (2024).

To see that this is the case, first return to the syllogistic argument of the *Intellectual Powers*. At first glance, it appears to be nothing more than a classic design argument. Militating against that interpretation, however, is what Reid writes concerning those who have defended the necessary first principle that every effect must have a cause. According to Reid,

> [w]e find Philosophers, ancient and modern, who can reason excellently in subjects that admit of reasoning, when they have occasion to defend this principle, not offering reasons for it, or any *medium* of proof, but appealing to the common sense of mankind; mentioning particular instances, to make the absurdity of the contrary opinion more apparent, and sometimes using wit and ridicule, which are very proper weapons for refuting absurdities, but altogether improper in points that are to be determined by reasoning. (Reid 2002a: 504–505, emphasis in the original)

In this passage, Reid makes clear that he thinks logical arguments are relatively useless against those who deny the necessary connection between cause and effect. In their stead, he recommends the giving of examples and the use of *reducio ad absurdum*. These, for him, are appeals to common sense. The need to defend first principles may initially seem strange. Doesn't Reid believe that it is a sign of first principles that they are nigh-universally accepted? Indeed he does. But this does not mean that *all* first principles are *always* believed. On the contrary, on account of the malign influence of the *idola* Bacon describes, we "may, to the end of life, be ignorant of" some "self-evident truths" (Reid 2010: 278). And, in the face of such errors, he argues that the best procedure for correcting our mistakes is to acquire a "clear, distinct and steady conception of the things about which we judge" (Reid 2010: 279).

Reid's belief that it is more important to bring someone who is wrong about a first principle into a position where they may clearly see the matter than to provide rational arguments also helps explain another feature of Reid's engagement with syllogistic design arguments that we have already noted: In the "Lectures on Natural Theology," Baird reports that Reid refused to endorse exactly the argument he gives in the *Intellectual Powers*. Yet it also highlights an apparent conflict between his presentation of the syllogistic design argument in the "Lectures" and the *Intellectual Powers*. Why, if Reid refused to endorse a syllogistic argument for the existence of God in the former, does he advance the same "argument from *final causes*" in the latter (Baird in Foster 2017: 76, emphasis in the original; see Reid 2002a: 509)?[14]

---

[14] Also, see his approving quotations of examples of design in Cicero and Tillotson in Reid (2002a: 505–506).

The answer, I believe, is that the syllogistic argument for the existence of God presented in the *Intellectual Powers* is a *reducio ad absurdum*, just not one that is directed toward the proposition that God exists. Shortly before introducing the syllogistic design argument in the *Intellectual Powers*, Reid writes that Hume has done something unprecedented: "Mr Hume, as far as I know, was the first that ever expressed any doubt" of the necessary first principles that caused things have a cause, and designed things have a designer (Reid 2002a: 499).[15] In order to respond to Hume's unusual objections, Reid must therefore do an unusual thing. And what he does is present the classic, syllogistic design argument, not for the purpose of showing that it is true, but for the purpose of showing that Hume's denial of the necessary major premise leads to absurdity. In other words, in the syllogistic design argument that appears in the *Intellectual Powers*, Reid is not assuming his major premise and minor premise are true in order to demonstrate existence of God; he is assuming that God exists and the marks of his design in the world are obvious in order to show that Hume must be wrong to question the necessary connection between evident design and the existence of designers.

Contrast this procedure with Reid's discussion of design in the "Lectures on Natural Theology." There, Baird reports that, when Reid came to demonstrate the existence of God on the basis of apparent design in nature, he chiefly proceeded by giving examples. Over the course of five lectures – that is, one-third of all his lectures on natural theology, and most of those dedicated to the existence of God – Reid provided example after example of what he believed to be evidences of grand and/or beautiful design in nature (see Baird in Foster 2017: 42–73). Further, insofar as he mentions the syllogistic argument also found in the *Intellectual Powers*, he does so only in passing and – as we have seen – without an endorsement (Reid 2002a: 504; Baird in Foster 2017: 76).

Indeed, I do not think that Reid actually endorses a design "argument," in the strict sense. The syllogism discussed in the *Intellectual Powers* is an argument, but is not intended to prove the existence of God. And the multiplication of examples in the "Lectures on Natural Theology" is not an argument at all. Of course, here we may ask, what of Reid's other design arguments: of the cosmological argument, argument from the near-universal belief in divinity and an afterlife, argument from the apparent contingency of the world, and argument based on miracles? Are these not also syllogistic arguments that

---

[15] Strictly, Reid is only here referring to Hume's doubt that all effects have causes. But Reid is clear that the positions are linked when he says that the metaphysical principle that things that evidence design have a designer "is opposed by the same author [i.e. Hume]" (Reid 2002a: 503).

show that Reid considered theism to be the result of an inference, or at least tried to boost its justification by rational argument? Except in the case of the cosmological argument, the evidence from surviving student notes is too scanty to describe Reid's procedure. With respect to the cosmological argument, we again find the evidence pointing away from the inferential interpretation and coherence account of the design argument. As Tuggy notes, although Reid discussed the cosmological argument in his lectures on natural theology, he completely abandoned the cosmological argument in the *Intellectual Powers* (Tuggy 2004: 293). Further, in the "Lectures on Natural Theology," he again appears to follow his own methodological advice. When he discusses the cosmological argument in the "Lectures on Natural Theology," Reid puts the cosmological arguments to two uses. First, Reid argues that the cosmological argument shows us that the creator, like creation, has "life, power, intelligence, and moral virtue" (Baird in Foster 2017: 39). This is an argument about the attributes of God and does not concern us here. Second, Reid argues that the belief that there is no first cause – that the causation of the universe is like "a chain hanging down from heaven," which has no first link – "appears to be a great absurdity" (Baird in Foster 2017: 39).

In other words, when Reid uses the cosmological argument to address the existence of God, he does so not to show that God exists, but as a *reducio* against atheism. In this way, Reid's use of the cosmological argument strengthens both the non-inferential interpretation and my interpretation of Reid's use of the design argument. He nowhere, it seems, uses a classic proof of God to either prove the existence of God or show the coherence of God's existence with first principles. Rather, insofar as he addresses such arguments about God's existence, he uses them to show that skepticism about first principles regarding necessary relations between cause and effect leads to absurdity.

This is not, however, to say that Reid thinks that the coherence of theism with other first principles is unimportant. My point here is just that Reid does not argue that the coherence of theism with other first principles is a reason to believe in God. On the contrary, as we will see in the next section, Reid thinks the coherence of theism with other first principles plays the opposite role. According to Reid, belief in the existence of God strengthens our belief in other first principles through theism's coherence with them.

3 The Function of Religion in Reid's Philosophy

In the previous section, I argued that the status question is best answered by the non-inferential interpretation. I also argued that, while I agree with Poore that

Reid believes first principles may sometimes be the conclusion of an inferential argument, and that such arguments may boost the justification of the proved first principles, I do not agree with Buras that Reid presents a design argument in order to boost confidence in theism. Rather, I think that Reid does not actually present a traditional design argument at all. In the *Intellectual Powers*, Reid uses a traditional, syllogistic design argument not for the purpose of proving the existence of God, but to show that the major premise of the argument – that designed things have a designer – is a true and necessary first principle. The syllogistic design argument discussed by Reid is, in other words, more of an illustration than an argument. Similarly, in the "Lectures on Natural Theology," Reid does not present and endorse a design argument as such. Although he mentions several arguments for the existence of God, his chief strategy for demonstrating the existence of God in the "Lectures" is to multiply examples of apparent design in nature in order to bring his students into the proper position to make a non-inferential judgment about the existence of God through the exercise of their sense of aesthetic taste. It remains to be seen, however, what role the non-inferential belief in the existence of God plays in Reid's philosophy. In this section, I will argue that Reid answers the function question in six distinct ways.

3.1 Theism and Trust in the External Senses

That theism is important to Reid is evident by his frequent references to God throughout his philosophical works. However, the exact function that belief in God's existence plays in his philosophy is curiously unclear. This is partly Reid's fault. Although he mentions God frequently, he nowhere tells us explicitly what functions these mentions are intended to play. Reid scholarship is therefore understandably divided on this issue.

So far, most of the scholarly interest regarding the function of theism in Reid's philosophy has focused on his epistemology, and especially on his account of the reliability of the external senses. According to Poore, there are chiefly three options that are commonly found in Reid scholarship. The first option holds that "Reid's major or only response to skeptical doubts regarding the reliability of our faculties is a dogmatic appeal to God" (Poore 2015: 216). Among the proponents of this interpretation, Poore lists Richard Popkin (1980), J. H. Faurot (1952), and Norman Daniels (1974) (Poore 2015: 217).[16] Yet this interpretation, as Poore notes, cannot be correct because Reid does not think that revelation is the only way that human beings can learn about the existence and

---

[16] As Di Ceglie (2020: 36n) and Rysiew (2002: 438) note, Daniels changed his mind between the first (1974) and second editions (1989) of his book on Reid and the geometry of the visibles.

nature of God. On the contrary, Poore writes, Reid "sees belief in God as grounded upon arguments" as well as on revelation (Poore 2015: 217). In the previous section, I argued that Reid thinks belief in God is grounded upon common sense, not arguments, but here they amount to the same thing because Reidian judgments of common sense are rational.

A second interpretation acknowledges that Reid believes theism can be rationally justified, but argues that his attempt to do so begs the question. Poore calls this interpretation of the relationship between Reid's belief in the existence of God and the reliability of our senses "vicious circularity" (Poore 2015: 217). According to this interpretation, endorsed by Sir Leslie Stephen (1902) and Ernest Sosa (2009), Reid justifies our belief in God on the basis of our judgments about the external world, and the veracity of our judgments about the external world on the basis of our God-given senses. This interpretation is an advance on the previous because it recognizes that Reid thinks theism ought to be assented to rationally, not simply dogmatically. Yet, as Poore points out, this second interpretation also cannot be true. For it to be true, it would have to be the case that Reid's only justification for belief in our senses is the existence of a good God who blesses us with reliable perceptions. Reid does indeed argue that our faculties of judgment are reliable because they are given by a good God, but, as discussed in Section 1, he also provides several arguments against the skeptic, which do not appeal to God. Or, as Poore puts it, since Reid's anti-skeptical arguments rely on an externalist epistemology that grounds first principles on non-inferential evidence, Reid "does not think we are justified in trusting our faculties *simply* because we believe a good God created us" (Poore 2015: 218).

The third interpretation Poore discusses holds that the existence of God is irrelevant to the justification of our external senses. According to James Somerville, for instance, Reid's references to God are "no more than pious reminders for the faithful" that have "no philosophical and certainly no epistemological significance" (Somerville 1995: 347; partially quoted in Poore 2015: 218). Yet this too is an implausible reading of Reid, for at least two reasons. First, while it is possible that Reid would reference the goodness of God among his discussions concerning the accuracy of our perceptions solely for the sake of providing "pious reminders," an interpretation so contrary to the plain meaning of the text requires ample evidence, which Somerville does not provide. Second, if we were correct in Section 2 that Reid thinks the existence of God is a first principle, it would be very odd if it provided no justification whatsoever for trusting our senses. After all, Reid believes that first principles are the foundation of all reasoning, and the existence of a good creator is clearly relevant to any discussion of the reliability of our intellectual faculties.

In contrast to these three interpretations, Poore provides a fourth according to which theism boosts our confidence in the veracity of our senses by means of coherence. The essential idea here is a simple one. According to Reid, the deliverances of our external senses do not typically require any more justification than is provided by their self-evidence. They are, themselves, first principles. Yet, because the apparent reliability of our external senses coheres with theism – and specifically belief in the existence of a good God who would not give us indefeasibly faulty external senses – their intuitive judgments of self-evidence are "boosted," making them "super-justified" (Poore 2015: 213, 224).

Poore believes that there need not be any circularity in the epistemic boosting provided by theism. In the case of the reliability of our external senses, however, I am not sure that this is correct. When describing the internal sense of taste – that is, our sensitivity to novelty, beauty, and grandeur – Reid distinguishes it from the external sense of taste – that is, our sensitivity to sapid bodies placed on our tongue – by writing "[o]ur external senses may discover qualities which do not depend on any antecedent perception. Thus I can hear the sound of a bell, though I never perceived any thing else belonging to it. But it is impossible to perceive the beauty of an object without perceiving the object, or at least conceiving it" (Reid 2002a: 578). Without the final clause, the case would be clear; the judgments of our internal sense of taste would be dependent on judgments about the perceptions of our external senses. With the last clause, however, Reid complicates the matter, especially because he admits that he does not have a good answer to the chicken-and-egg problem created by his simultaneous assertion that (1) judgments rely upon conceptions and (2) all conceptions are products of judgment. Is Reid here claiming that the conceptions that form the evidence from which the internal sense of taste makes its judgments are the products of the judgments of our external senses, or would he allow that the internal sense of taste could operate on some of the mysterious, early conceptions whose origins "like the sources of the Nile" are unknown (Reid 2002a: 416)?

If the answer is the latter, then Poore is correct that there may be no circularity in the boosting function of theism in Reid. If the answer is the former, there is. Yet it need not be vicious. There is a kind of virtuous circularity in coherence that raises our confidence about already-justified beliefs, as we have seen in the case of Dr. Saunderson's proofs regarding the geometry of objects viewed in perspective. If our geometry yielded conclusions that strongly contradicted our sense perceptions, we would think that something had gone wrong. The fact that our perceptions and geometry do cohere, however, can be taken as a sign that both are reliable, despite the (at least partial) dependence of geometry on our senses of sight and touch.

Yet, even if Poore is wrong to say that there is no circularity here, his general account of the boosting function of theism appears to be the best characterization of the function of theism in Reid's account of the external senses, for two reasons. First, it avoids the excesses and elisions of the previous versions. Reid does not treat theistic belief as a dogmatic foundation for other beliefs, as the only rational justification for the reliability of our external senses, or as irrelevant. And second, it chimes with Reid's most explicit description of the relationship between theism and our belief in the reliability of our external senses:

> Shall we say then that the belief [in the accuracy of our external senses] is the inspiration of the Almighty? I think this may be said in a good sense; for I take it to be the immediate effect of our constitution, which is the work of the Almighty. But if inspiration be understood to imply a persuasion of its coming from God, our belief of the objects of sense is not inspiration, *for a man would believe his senses though he had no notion of a Deity.* He who is persuaded that he is the workmanship of God, and that it is a part of his constitution to believe his senses, *may think that a good reason to confirm his belief.* But he had the belief before he could give this or any other reason for it. (Reid 2002a: 231–232, emphases added)

Following Reid's reasoning here, it seems that the use of theism to boost confidence in our external senses can be generalized to all of what Reid calls our "intellectual powers": our faculties of memory, apprehension, abstraction, judgment, reasoning, and aesthetic taste. Like our external senses, all these also are, according to Reid, natural and instinctive intellective powers of the human mind, and their reliability, though self-evident and thus not solely justified by an appeal to the existence of a good God, coheres with a belief in the same. This being the case, we have one answer to the function question. With regard to our powers of understanding, theism does not justify our common-sense beliefs or our trust in our natural mental faculties, but it boosts confidence in them by showing their coherence with a divinely ordered world. In other words, theism provides internalist confirmation of our externally justified common-sense beliefs by adding a reason to the already-sufficient (self-)evidence of their reliability (see also Poore 2015: 226).

3.2 Theism and the Rational Powers of Action

According to Reid, in addition to the purely intellectual powers just discussed, human beings have active powers, some of which are also intellective. These intellectual and active powers he calls "rational principles of action" (Reid 2010: 152). We have already seen that Reid thinks theism plays an important epistemological role in boosting our confidence in our purely intellective powers. It seems natural, therefore, to ask: Does theism play a similar epistemological role in Reid's account of the rational powers of action?

To answer this question, we must first say a bit about Reid's understanding of the rational active powers, and active powers in general. Generally, Reid divided the active powers into three types. The first and most basic kind are called "mechanical principles." These are principles that operate automatically, like instinctual respiration and unintentional blinking (see Reid 2010: 75–91). The second are what he calls "animal principles." These principles operate according to "will and intention" and include all our appetites, desires, and passions (Reid 2010: 92). In lower animals and infants, only mechanical principles are found. In higher animals and young children, we find both mechanical and animal principles at work. In mature human beings, however, we also find a third type of active principle that Reid calls "rational" because "they can exist only in beings endowed with reason, and because, to act from these principles, is what has always been meant by acting according to reason" (Reid 2010: 153).

According to Reid, there are two rational principles of action. The first is what he calls our "good on the whole," and which he defines as "that which, taken with all its discoverable connections and consequences, brings more good than ill" (Reid 2010: 155). What Reid has in mind here is a rational assessment of those things in life that tend toward our happiness, including the ability to compare the relative goodness or badness of certain courses of action as well as the challenges or durations that stand between us and achieving them. This principle therefore considers the impulses given to us by our animal principles – our appetites, passions, and desires – and also rules over them to bring about a rationally ordered life.

> To prefer a greater good, though distant, to a less that is present; to chuse a present evil, in order to avoid a greater evil, or to obtain a greater good, is, in the judgment of all men, wise and reasonable conduct ... Nor will it be denied, that, in innumerable cases in common life, our animal principles draw us one way, while a regard to what is good on the whole draws us the contrary way ... That in every conflict of this kind the rational principle ought to prevail, and the animal be subordinate, is too evident to need, or to admit of proof. (Reid 2010: 156)

The second rational principle of action Reid calls "duty." And, in contrast with our good on the whole, this principle stands apart from our animal principles because it "cannot be resolved into that of interest, or what is most for our happiness" (Reid 2010: 169). This is because duty, for Reid, forbids and commands certain actions categorically. Much could, and has, been said about Reid's account of these principles of action.[17] Here, however, we are chiefly interested in the way theism interacts with them.

According to some interpreters, theism plays a crucial role in Reid's account of the second rational principle of action. Quoting from the *Active Powers*, where Reid writes that "the conscience which is in every man's breast is the law of God written in his heart," Knud Haakonssen remarks that, for Reid, "morality is an elaborate network of 'offices' of greatly varying extent to which God has appointed us" (Haakonssen in Reid 1990: liv–lv; Reid 2010: 365). Similarly, James Harris writes that there "is nothing more basic to which the experience of conscience might be reduced, and no means of explaining why conscience operates as it does, except through direct appeal to the ultimately inscrutable intentions of the divine mind itself" (Harris 2010: 221). For Haakonssen and Harris, theism is essential to Reid's account of duty.

There is ample textual support for the close association between duty and God's will in Reid (see, e.g., Reid 2010: 192, 229, 273, 304, 622). However, he also, at times, distinguishes them. For example, in an unpublished manuscript, Reid explicitly distinguishes divine sanction and duty when he writes that systems that "resolve all Moral Obligation into the Will of God" are "at bottom the Same as the Selfish System," by which he means ethical systems that counsel not duty but the pursuit of self-interest (Reid, AUL MS 2131 7/II/7, p. 5; quoted in Reid 2010: 159 n). As Reid's endorsement of our "good on the whole" as a rational principle of action shows, Reid does not reject self-interest, but this note indicates that Reid did not always reduce our duties to God's will, or conflate the operation of our conscience with God's inspiration.

Of course, when considering the relationship between theism and duty in Reid, we ought to be wary of overemphasizing the importance of a single line in an unpublished manuscript. Yet, while Reid frequently acknowledges that duty is always compatible with the divine will, he gives us other reasons for thinking that duty is not simply reducible to the dictates of God. Consider, for example, Reid's definition of duty in the *Active Powers*. There, he writes that duty is "what we ought to do, what is fair and honest, what is approvable, what every man professes to be the rule of his conduct, what all men praise, and what is it, though no man should praise," and further explains that it is a necessary objective relation between an agent and an action within a community of rational agents (Reid 2010: 169). In this definition, the divine will is conspicuously absent. Similarly, when Reid defends the concept of duty against the

---

[17] See especially Rowe (1991), Davis (2006), and Foster (2024). Roeser (2010) is also an excellent resource.

subjectivist arguments of Hume, he chiefly does so not on the grounds that it is God's will, but on the ground that duty is a necessary, practical relation among autonomous agents and actions. Reid's defense of the faculty by which we perceive our duties moves along the same lines. When Reid describes our conscience or "moral sense," he treats it as a faculty of judgment that, like our external senses, instinctively and reliably renders first principles of morals upon the apprehension of self-evidence (see Reid 2010: 174–180). We therefore ought not be misled when Reid writes that, for example, our conscience is "the candle of the LORD set up within us" (Reid 2010: 192). For Reid, our moral sense is a common-sense faculty of judgment instilled in us by our creator. All going well, our moral sense – no less than our external senses – is a faculty that makes accurate judgments on the basis of self-evidence, without needing any special appeal to the existence of, or inspiration from, God.

This is not to say, however, that theism plays no role in Reid's account of ethics. According to Reid, "[r]ight sentiments of the Deity and his works . . . add the authority of a Divine law to every rule of right conduct" (Reid 2010: 276).[18] This, in so many words, is an endorsement of Poore's coherence account of the function of theism in Reid's epistemology, applied to his ethics. And it gives us a second function of theism, in direct parallel with the first. As with the external senses, a well-functioning conscience is fully capable of making reliable, common-sense judgments based on self-evidence. However, when we recognize these judgments are also the sanctions of divine law, we have yet a further reason to trust that our moral judgments are justified and our moral sense is operating correctly.

A third way that theism plays a role in the operation of our rational powers of action, according to Reid, is by giving us another, and especially important, member of the moral community: namely, God. In his "Lectures and Papers on Practical Ethics," Reid divides his presentation of our duties according to the ancient tradition of duties to God, self, and others. The relation of theism to the first of these divisions is obvious. If God is a member of the moral community, there are duties owed to God, and specifically, according to Reid, our affection, our attention, and our adherence to the rational moral law, which God, as a perfect moral agent, perfectly wills (see Reid 2007: 17–23). Intriguingly, Reid also suggests that God may stand behind the second division as well. As Reid sees it, we are obliged to cultivate our talents because "[a]ll the powers & abilities of body & mind fortune or Station which a man is possessed of by Nature, or may acquire by his industry are the talents which God has given him"

---

[18] Note that, idiosyncratically for Reid, "sentiment" means "judgment accompanied by feeling," not just an affective response (Reid 2010: 353).

(Reid 2007: 26). Therefore, although we "cannot indeed profit our maker by the right use of these talents ... we may please him and deserve his approbation, and may greatly profit ourselves and our fellow creatures, by using our talents in a right manner" (Reid 2007: 26). On one reading, then, all "duties to ourselves" are, at bottom, duties to God. Complicating this purely theistic understanding of our duties to ourselves, however, is what Reid says next. Immediately after making the connection between our duties to ourselves and God, he adds the caveat that "if we had no Account to make to God, our own Conscience must condemn us" (Reid 2007: 26). It is therefore not clear whether Reid thinks theism is necessary to rationally affirm that there are duties to ourselves. On the one hand, Reid seems to say that we ought to cultivate our talents because they are the gift of God. On the other, he also indicates that cultivating our talents is immediately commanded by the moral sense (see also Reid 2010: 274). If the latter is correct, then theism is only required to make rational judgments about duties to God, and plays, at best, a super-justifying role with respect to duties to ourselves.

Whatever the case with respect to duties to ourselves, we find a fourth function of theism in Reid's account of the connection between our two rational principles of action. According to Reid, although both "good on the whole" and "duty" are "two distinct principles of action," "both suppose the use of reason, and when rightly understood, both lead to the same course of life"; they are therefore "like two fountains whose streams unite and run in the same channel" (Reid 2010: 173). As Reid believes that truth is always consistent with itself, the coincidence of these two rational principles of action is necessary. They cannot, by his lights, both be rational and yet point in opposing directions. Yet, although Reid affirms the coincidence of our two rational principles of action and believes that we typically perceive no conflict between these two principles, he is also aware that there are times when acting according to duty and securing our good on the whole seem to conflict. Take, for example, someone who lives in a corrupt society where they can only secure the material goods necessary to sustain life by paying bribes or acting as an informant for malicious government forces. In such a state, it may seem that to act according to duty is simply not to pursue one's good on the whole, and vice versa. It is in response to cases like these, when our two rational principles of action seem to conflict, that Reid deploys an appeal to God. As Reid puts it, "[w]hile the world is under a wise and benevolent administration, it is impossible, that any man should ... be a loser by doing his duty. Every man, therefore, who believes in God, while he is careful to do his duty, may safely leave the care of his happiness to him who made him" (Reid 2010: 194; see also Reid 2007: 21–22). For a nontheist in such a situation, on the other hand, "it will be impossible for the man to act, so as not to contradict a leading principle of his nature. He must either sacrifice his happiness to virtue, or virtue to happiness; and is reduced to this miserable dilemma, whether it be best to be a fool or a knave" (Reid 2010: 194). Thus, according to Reid, "I cannot help thinking that such Virtue as disdains any aid of Religion stands upon a very slippery foundation, & will hardly be able to endure any severe trial" (Reid 2007: 23).

This fourth function of theism is a type of super-justification, but I have listed it separately from the first and second functions because it seems to operate in a different way than Poore describes. In those former functions, theism boosts our confidence in the judgments of our intellectual powers and rational active powers individually by directly cohering with them. In this fourth function, theism again bolsters the judgments of our rational active powers. Yet it does so not by direct confirmation, but by requiring that both rational principles always coincide. Thus, for Reid, theism doesn't just agree with our rational principles of action. It also forms a rational bridge between them.

3.3 Theism and Motivation

So far, our discussion of theism's effect on the active powers has focused on the intellective aspect of the rational powers. Yet none of our active powers, according to Reid, are, or could be, purely intellective. They must also motivate us to action. Does theism, then, have any motivational function through its influence on our active powers? According to Reid, it has two. First, theism affects our motivations by influencing our rational principles. And second, theism inspires animal motives.

To understand how theism can motivate us in these ways, it is first necessary to say a bit about how Reid thinks we are motivated to act. Being a libertarian with respect to free will, Reid thinks that the actions of properly functioning human beings are never determined by motives. For him, we are the cause of our own actions because we have the ability to choose among various motives, or even act without a motive (see Reid 2010: 47–59). Yet we are influenced by motives. The first type are animal motives, which are the product of our animal principles of action. These motives, like hunger, fear, or affection push us toward or pull us away from certain actions without a rational consideration of their ends. Higher animals, young children, and people without reason are ruled by these motives: They always act according to the strongest animal motive present at a given time. Well-functioning rational agents, on the other hand, do not. They may, by means of their rational faculties, choose among their animal motives, or choose against them all (see Reid 2010: 53). They are also influenced by the second type of motive Reid describes: rational motives. These do not influence our will by "blind impulse as animal motives do," but rather by means of rational conviction that certain ends are compatible with, or required or forbidden by, our rational judgments concerning duty and good on the whole (Reid 2010: 219).[19]

The first way that theism affects our motivations, according to Reid, follows straightforwardly from the description of rational motives and what has already been said regarding theism's ability to boost the certainty of our judgments about our good on the whole and duty. Our rational powers of action are both intellectual and active powers. They are intellectual in the sense that they are faculties of judgment. They are active in the sense that they influence our will by presenting to it rational motives. Therefore, just as theism makes our judgments regarding good on the whole and duty more certain, so it simultaneously makes the pursuit of those ends more convincing to our free will. And this is especially true for people who are confident that, by doing their duty, they also always pursue their good on the whole, since they will be less likely to abandon the former for the sake of the latter in difficult times.

The second way that theism affects our motivations is by stirring up animal affections. In the previous section, we saw that Reid draws a close connection between aesthetic perception and belief in God. God, for Reid, is the great architect of the universe whose works inspire an aesthetic appreciation both of themselves and of God's excellence. And this appreciation is not, for Reid, merely intellectual. It is also accompanied by motivating animal affections. Some of these, according to Reid, coincide with our rational motives regarding our good on the whole and duty. As he writes in the *Intellectual Powers*, "[t]he emotion which this grandest of all objects raises in the human mind, is what we call devotion; a serious recollected temper which inspires magnanimity, and disposes to the most heroic acts of virtue" (Reid 2002a: 582). According to Reid, virtuous animal motives such as these are helpful in our pursuit of rational ends because rational motives are often opposed by animal motives. We may, for example, believe it is our duty to perform some task, but feel disinclined to perform it because it is difficult. In such a case, our rational motive is opposed by an animal desire for ease. If, however, the nonvirtuous desire for ease is itself opposed by a virtuous animal affection for doing God's will, we will find it easier to perform our duty. The virtuous animal motive, in a sense, aids our rational motive, by giving us a "blind impulse" that coincides with it.[20]

---

[19] For an excellent discussion of Reid's complex account of motives, see Cuneo (2020) in this series.

[20] For a discussion on Reid's account of the relationship between rational motives and coincident animal motives, see Kroeker (2011).

In addition to stirring up virtuous animal motives, Reid also believes that theism inspires animal motives that incline us toward the study of nature. As we discussed in Section 1, although Reid is chiefly known today for his work in epistemology and ethics, his interests were broad. His passionate interests in biology, agriculture, mathematics, astronomy, and botany are all evident from his extant papers. No doubt some of Reid's energy and interest in all things philosophical and scientific came from his natural disposition. But, as Wood writes, Reid's "insatiable appetite for the study of God's creation" – his polymathic attitude toward the study of nature – was also "fueled by his religious sensibilities" (Wood "Introduction" in Reid 1995: 18–19).

The evidence that Reid was inspired by his theism to study the natural world is often explicit. Throughout his work, we find Reid constantly praising God's creativity and craftsmanship. According to Reid, "[t]his grand machine of the natural world displays the power and wisdom of the artificer" (Reid 2010: 226). Similarly, the study of the natural world leads "us only to admire the wisdom of the Creator" (Reid 2010: 122). Therefore, when "we attend to the marks of good contrivance which appear in the works of God, every discovery we make in the constitution of the material or intellectual system becomes a hymn of praise to the great Creator and Governor of the World" (Reid 2002a: 509). This last quotation is especially significant because Baird records a nearly identical quotation in his notes on Reid's natural theology lectures.[21] It seems, then, that the "we" in the phrase "we attend" is not just polite authorial distancing. Reid is not only reporting his own motivations; he is also attempting to inspire the same appreciation for the grandeur and beauty of the universe in his students and readers, so that they too will undertake the hard work of deciphering the laws of nature.

Thus, in sum, theism plays at least six important roles in Reid's philosophy. First, it boosts our confidence in the non-inferential common-sense judgments of our intellective powers. Second, it does the same for the judgments of our rational active powers. Third, it provides to us another and important member of the moral community to whom duties are owed. Fourth, it assures us that the two rational principles of action – good on the whole and duty – always recommend the same course of action. Fifth, it helps to motivate us toward ends that align with our good on the whole and duty by increasing our confidence in our rational practical judgments. And sixth, it inspires animal motives that induce us to follow our rational principles and study the natural world.

---

[21] "Indeed, when we attend to the marks of wisdom and intelligence that appear all around, every discovery proves a new hymn of praise to him who is the creator and governor of the world" (Baird in Foster 2017: 76).

4 The Question of Detachability

In the previous section, we saw that theism plays several roles in Reid's account of the intellectual and active powers. In this section, we address a final question regarding Reid's theism: Is it detachable from Reid's philosophy? In his article "Revisiting Reid on Religion," Buras asks several questions under the aegis of what he calls the "detachability question": "Can [Reid's theistic statements] be dismissed . . . as pious irrelevancies? Are they meant to have some philosophical relevance? If so, are they capable of getting the job done, and are they required to get the job done?" (Buras 2021: 268–269). In Sections 2 and 3, we have already answered the first two of these queries and seen that theism plays several important roles in Reid's philosophy. In this section, we address modified versions of the latter two questions, which I believe to be the heart of the detachability question. First, does Reid think that nontheists can be rational agents? And second, what is lost from Reid's philosophy if we remove theism from it?

4.1 Theism and Rationality in Reid

The question "does Reid think theism is necessary for rationality?" can be asked at three separate levels. First, does Reid think that one must be a theist to be a basic rational agent, someone who has that degree of Reidian common sense "which is necessary to our being subjects of law and government, capable of managing our own affairs, and answerable for our conduct towards others" (Reid 2002a: 426)? Second, does Reid believe that one must be a theist to rationally engage in Baconian science? And third, does Reid believe that one must be a theist to rationally pursue philosophy in general? Despite the several functions that theism plays in Reid's philosophy, to a surprising extent, the answer to all these questions is negative. In the preceding sections, we have already seen three reasons why. First, at the level of basic human rationality, Reid argues that our knowledge is built upon a broad foundation of non-inferential first principles justified by self-evidence. Thus, as we saw in Sections 1, 2, and 3, while the addition of theism may boost our confidence in these common-sense judgments, they are justified apart from theism.

Second, with regard to the study of the natural world, Reid follows Bacon's dictum that science seeks only to catalogue the regularities of nature, and not to speculate about the active agent or agents behind them. Indeed, so adamant is Reid regarding the exclusion of causal agents from his natural philosophy that he cannot accept his philosophical hero Newton's theological speculations when they function as explanations of natural phenomena. According to the *Intellectual Powers*, "ISAAC NEWTON thought, that the Deity, by existing every where, and at all times, constitutes time and space, immensity and eternity" (Reid 2002a: 261).[22] This is, according to Reid, the speculation of a man of "superior genius"; yet he refuses to endorse it, writing that whether it be "as solid as [it] is sublime, or … the wanderings of imagination in a region beyond the limits of human understanding, I am unable to determine" (Reid 2002a: 261; see also Reid 2002b: 146–147).

Third, regarding the areas of philosophical investigation for which Reid believes a Baconian approach is inappropriate – "Morals, Jurisprudence, Natural Theology, and the abstract Sciences of Mathematicks and Metaphysicks" – only Natural Theology seems to rationally require theism, according to Reid (1995: 185–186). This is because all of the other branches of non-Baconian investigation stand upon their own set of non-inferential and nontheistic first principles. It is true and natural, of course, that if you accept theism, then God will play a role in your jurisprudence, morals, metaphysics, and even mathematics. Their truths will be the will of God. But if one does not, then they will still be founded upon necessary first principles (see Reid 2002a: 495). Take, for example, Reid's attempt to list the first principles of morals in the *Active Powers*. While several include a mention of God in their explanation, only one includes God in the principle itself, and here only in the form of a conditional: "To every man who believes the existence, the perfections, and the providence of GOD the veneration and submission we owe to him is self-evident" (Reid 2010: 276). The implication is clear. While Reid believes nontheists are incorrect, that God exists, and that we do in fact owe to God certain duties, he also holds that the only duties that rationally require assent to the existence of God are those duties that are owed to God.

4.2 The Role of Theism in Aesthetic Taste

If this is correct, then we may answer the fist question regarding Reids understanding of the relationship between theism and rationality – whether Reid thinks nontheists can be rational – affirmatively. Yet, before we can move to the question of what, for Reid, is lost by not believing in God, it is necessary to address one objection by Rachel Zuckert. The issue – which Zuckert terms the "God-problem" – is this: As Reid is adamant that belief in a divine creator is part and parcel with an appreciation for natural beauty – so adamant, in fact, that the perception of natural grandeur and beauty leads to the first principle that God exists – it seems that we cannot separate the one from the other (Zuckert 2015: 155; see also Buras 2021: 271). For Reid, perceptions of original grandeur and beauty in nature just are perceptions that God exists. What, then, can Reid say

---

[22] See also Callergård (2010: 114–116).

about atheistic perceptions of natural grandeur and beauty? It seems there are three possibilities. For Reid, they will be impossible, fraudulent, or diminished.

The first possibility is that, without a simultaneous belief in the existence of God, the perception of natural grandeur and beauty is impossible. This is not a plausible solution simply because people without theistic commitments do, in fact, perceive grandeur and beauty in nature. And Reid would agree. Although he considers Hume to be an agnostic at best, and questions Hume's theory of beauty, he nowhere questions Hume's perception of natural beauty. Nor, to turn the problem around, does he imply that Hume actually does believe in God because he can perceive beauty in nature. The fact that Reid does not accuse Hume of unspoken theistic belief here is notable because it contrasts with his arguments that Hume does not live up to his skepticism (see Reid 2002a: 571; Reid 2003: 20). And it indicates that, while Reid thinks we cannot avoid madness without implicitly trusting our basic common-sense judgments, he doesn't think perceptions of natural grandeur and beauty always require belief in God.

A second option is to suppose that, according to Reid, if God does not exist, then all perceptions of grandeur and beauty in nature are misleading. This option is internally consistent. If nature has no creator, then its (apparent) excellence could not reflect the excellence of the mind that made it. It therefore could not actually be grand or beautiful, and any judgments about natural grandeur and beauty would be errors. Copenhaver gives a plausible account of how mistakes of this type might happen. Perhaps our tendency to correctly associate grand and beautiful artifacts with the excellence of the minds that made them misleads us into thinking that similar natural objects were also intentionally created (Copenhaver 2015: 135). This interpretation chimes with some recent accounts of human psychology. For example, Justin Barrett has proposed that human beings have what he calls a "hypersensitive agent detection device," which, for evolutionary reasons, is liable to produce belief in the existence of agents from ambiguous signs where there are none (Barrett 2004: 32). Yet, while this option is a philosophical possibility, I think that such a stance does not so much detach Reid's theology from his epistemology as reject Reid's account of aesthetic taste.

The problem is this: From a Reidian perspective, once we take the line that the apparent grandeur and beauty of nature is counterfeit, we cannot still treat it as actual. Zuckert considers the opposite approach when she speculatively suggests that, because it resembles actual beauty, we may pay "homage" to apparent but false natural beauty even though it is not derived of any original beauty (Zuckert 2015: 158). This too is philosophically plausible, but it does not seem to be amenable to Reid's own position. As he says when considering the alleged fallacy of the senses:

> When a man has taken a counterfeit guinea for a true one, he says his sense deceived him; but he lays the blame where it ought not be laid: For we may ask him, Did your senses give a false testimony of the colour, or of the figure, or the of the impression? No. But this is all that they testified, and this they testified truly: From these premises you concluded that it was a true guinea, but this conclusion does not follow; you erred therefore, not by relying upon the testimony of sense, but by judging rashly from its testimony: Not only are your senses innocent of this error, but it is only by their information that it can be discovered. If you consult them properly, they will inform you that what you took for a guinea is base metal, or is deficient in weight, and this can only be known by the testimony of sense. (Reid 2002a: 244)

Applying this scheme to the sense of aesthetic taste, it will either be the case that we find we can, upon closer examination, detect some defect in the works of nature, which makes them less than grand or beautiful, or that the sense of aesthetic taste renders irresistible judgments about the excellence and existence of nature's creator, which are clearly contradicted by the testimony of some other senses or rational arguments. This is a choice between treating the wonders of nature with the same derision as a counterfeit coin or deciding that our sense of aesthetic taste is incorrigibly fallacious. The first option, from Reid's point of view, is flatly contradicted by the universal opinion in all cultures and times that nature is grand and beautiful. The second assumes an indefeasible defect in one of our senses. Both options therefore posit errors too large to be accommodated by Reid's epistemology (see Reid 2002a: 595).

There is a third option, however, which shows that Reid's theism is at least partially detachable from his account of aesthetic taste. This option makes careful use of Reid's distinction between derived and original grandeur and beauty. As we saw in Section 2, for Reid, the original grandeur and beauty evidenced by an object is an objective excellence; specifically, it is the excellence of the mind that made it. But derived grandeur and beauty is likewise objective for Reid: "[T]he object has its excellence from its own constitution and not from ours" (Reid 2002a: 587; see Copenhaver 2015: 135 although cf. Jaffro 2015: 170–173). This derived excellence is not the same as the excellence of the mind that made it, but it is an expression of that excellence: It bears the excellent mind's "signature," to use Reid's language. Or, to put it in Zuckert's apt formulation, for Reid, the excellence of derived grandeur and beauty "points beyond itself" (Zuckert 2015: 158).

What it points to, however, is not always clear. But this does not mean that the object itself cannot be grand or beautiful. After all, encountering derived beauty but being unable to trace it back to the original beauty of its creator's mind is not an uncommon challenge. The authorship of many human works is contested. And the experience of wondering whether a certain grand or beautiful object or sound was made by a person or by nature is not uncommon.

Reid, of course, thinks that the evidence of natural grandeur and beauty is enough to warrant theism. For him, they point, like the finger of John the Baptist, to God. We may, though, stay within the confines of Reid's philosophy without accepting Reid's judgment here by appealing to another distinction Reid makes in his account of aesthetic taste. As we noted in Section 2, and paralleling the difference between derived and original beauty on the objective side, Reid makes a distinction between "instinctive" and "rational" aesthetic taste on the subjective.

By contrasting the instinctive with the rational here, Reid does not mean to say that instinctive judgments of aesthetic taste are irrational. Instinctive judgments of beauty are still judgments, and therefore still rational in the same way that instinctive perceptions of the external world are rational to Reid. They are self-evident first principles, upon which we may reason. But rational aesthetic judgments differ from instinctive in the sense that they are reflective; they are not only judgments that an object is beautiful but are judgments that are "grounded on some agreeable quality of the object which is distinctly conceived, and may be specified" (Reid 2002a: 598). To illustrate the difference between these, Reid provides the following example:

> In a heap of pebbles, one that is remarkable for brilliancy of color, and regularity of figure, will be picked out of the heap by a child. He perceives a beauty in it, puts a value upon it, and is fond of the property of it. For this preference, no reason can be given, but that children are, by their constitution, fond of brilliant colours, and of regular figures.

> Suppose again that an expert mechanic views a well constructed machine. He sees all its parts to be made of the fittest materials, and of the most proper form; nothing superfluous, nothing deficient; every part adapted to its use, and the whole fitted in the most perfect manner to the end for which it is intended. He pronounces it to be a beautiful machine. He views it with the same agreeable emotion as the child viewed the pebble; but he can give a reason for his judgment, and point out the particular perfections of the object on which it is grounded. (Reid 2002a: 598)

The close relation between Reid's account of aesthetic taste and his rational justification of theism are readily apparent in this passage. But the contrast between "instinctive" and "rational" aesthetic taste also allows Reid to account for true, nontheistic judgments of natural grandeur and beauty. As Copenhaver notes, there is a connection for Reid between instinctive aesthetic taste and derived grandeur and beauty on the one hand, and rational aesthetic taste and original grandeur and beauty on the other.[23] If this is the case, then, on Reid's account, all judgments of natural beauty by nontheists are instinctive, while the judgments of natural grandeur and beauty by theists can be both instinctive and rational.

One implication of this view is that, on Reid's account, as soon as nontheists begin to reflect on the grandeur and beauty of nature – as soon as they begin to move from an instinctive to a reflective judgment – theism becomes rationally required. This, however, does not mean that nontheists who reflect on their aesthetic appreciation of nature will actually believe in God. For, as we have seen, Reid is well aware that human beings do not assent to every true and justified proposition; even those that he believes to be self-evident.

4.3 What is Lost in Reid without Theism?

If these conclusions are correct, then, with the noted exception of rational aesthetic taste, theism is largely detachable from Reid's philosophy. Yet this prompts an obvious question: If Reid does not think that one must be a theist to be a rational or moral agent, a Baconian scientist, or, more generally, a philosopher to correctly judge that nature is grand and beautiful, then what is lost without theism? Using our answers to the function question in Section 3, we may easily assemble a list: First and second, according to Reid, nontheists are more prone than theists to skepticism without the super-justification that belief in God gives to the deliverances of our intellectual powers and the intellective aspects of our rational active powers. Third, nontheists also, by definition, do not believe they owe to God the performance of any duties, possibly including duties owed to ourselves. Fourth and fifth, they are also more likely to act contrary to duty without the assurance that our good on the whole and duty always concur, and without the aid of the virtuous animal principles Reid believes theism inspires. And sixth, according to Reid, they lack the motivation that reverence for God's creative power brings to the study of the natural world.

Looking at this list of losses, it does not seem likely that any nontheist will be moved to reconsider theism from a cost–benefit standpoint. Reid himself acknowledges that actual skepticism about our intellectual powers is vanishingly rare, if not actually impossible. Likewise, theism is not, according to Reid, the only or even chief support of our moral sense, nor the only inspiration for studying the natural world. For there are clearly many reasons to study the

---

[23] I am not as confident as Copenhaver that rational aesthetic taste never regards derived beauty. For an alternative account see Jaffro (2015: 172).

natural world, including the Baconian admonition to use discoveries in science for "human progress and empowerment" (Bacon 2002: 13). Nor is it likely that nontheists would acutely feel the loss of duties to a being they do not believe exists. Indeed, the only significant loss from the nontheistic perspective is the one just discussed regarding natural beauty. According to Reid, nontheists lack a rational account of why nature is beautiful and must therefore be satisfied with only the instinctive judgment that it is.

Yet these losses appear more severe when one considers the epistemic austerity of Reid's philosophy. It is not true, as it has sometimes been alleged, that Reid merely takes the inverse of Hume's position; that "Reid bawled out, We must believe in an outward world; but added in a whisper, We can give no reason for our belief" (Mackintosh 1846: 174a). As we saw in the first section, Reid thinks belief in the external world is not only rationally justified but rationally required. However, despite Reid's insistence on this point, and his zeal for cataloging the regularities of nature, Reid's Baconian commitment to the exclusion of any discussion of agency within nature generates a spartan intellectual world of pure phenomena without (in Reid's sense) causal explanation. Indeed, so spare is this Baconian world of pure, regular phenomena that Wolterstorff has proposed "left in darkness" as an appropriate motto for Reid's philosophy (Reid 2010: 30; Wolterstorff 2004: 83; see also Reid 2002a: 226).

This is not, necessarily, a problem. Perhaps, if we were different types of beings, we could live with such a universe: a universe in which we accepted the bare fact of natural law and the objective but unaccountable grandeur and beauty of the universe without yearning for an explanation. Perhaps if we were different, we could be satisfied with causal aporia. But, according to Reid, it so happens that we are beings who have a natural and ineluctable "avidity to know the causes of things," by which he means the true causes: the agent or agents behind phenomena and the ends to which they are directed (Reid 2002a: 100).

The austerity of Reid's Baconian universe thus puts nontheists in a bind. One of three things must break to relieve it. Our science must give us more, we must resign ourselves to never fulfilling our natural desire to know causes, or we must assent to the existence of God. Wood has suggested that, in some instances at least, Reid overstates the strictness of Baconian science. In his introduction to Reid's papers on animate creation, Wood writes that "Reid was all too willing to withdraw into a posture of nescience about the processes involved in reproduction in order to protect his religious beliefs" (Wood in Reid 1995: 19). This may be true.[24] Yet whether or not a Baconian investigation of the universe may yield

---

[24] Although, cf. Di Ceglie (2020: 33–34).

more explanation than Reid grants in some areas, it seems clear that, for Reid, it cannot give us answers to the deepest questions in philosophy. It cannot give us causality. Absent, then, a change in the natural desires of human beings, the tension between what we wish to ask and what Reid believes Baconian science can tell is, for him, real.

I do not intend here to propose a solution to this tension, either for or against the theists. But we may close by noting that if, for Reid, there are questions prompted by Baconian investigation that only theology can answer, then we have, at last, a good answer for the question that underlies this little Element, and indeed any discussion of Reid's religion: Why does Reid – the avowed champion of Baconianism – mention God so frequently in his philosophical works? In Section 1, we gave the partial answer that, in studying the human mind, Reid inevitably finds himself accounting for the fact that most human beings believe in God. If our discussion since then has been correct, we may substantially supplement that answer with the observation that Reid's Baconian investigations keep bumping into questions of causality, for which only theology is sufficient.

He could, of course, have merely ignored these questions, and kept all discussions of efficient and final causes out of his natural philosophy; and by doing so, he would have maintained the Baconian purity of his investigations. But, while Reid is keen not to give theological answers to Baconian questions, such a strict sequestration would seem to overemphasize the separation between natural philosophy and natural theology. It would also be contrary to the example of Newton. As Reid wrote to his friend and patron Lord Kames regarding Newton, if "in Scholia and Queries [of the *Principia*] he gives a Range to his thoughts, & sometimes enters into the Regions of Natural Theology & Metaphysics, this I think was very allowable" (Reid 2002b: 147). After all, when we observe the regularities, grandeur, and beauty of the universe, and inquire about our place within it, it is only natural to want both an accurate account of nature's laws and an answer to the causal question "why"? And there is further connection too. Although the methodologies of natural philosophy and natural theology are different, both for Reid are founded upon principles of common sense.

References

Ahnert, Thomas (2014) *The Moral Culture of the Scottish Enlightenment, 1690–1805*. New Haven, CT: Yale University Press (The Lewis Walpole Series in Eighteenth-Century Culture and History).

Bacon, Francis (2002) *The New Organon*. Edited by L. Jardine and M. Silverthorne. Cambridge: Cambridge University Press (Cambridge Texts in the History of Philosophy).

Barrett, Justin L. (2004) *Why Would Anyone Believe in God?* Walnut Creek, CA: AltaMira Press.

Buras, Todd (2021) "Revisiting Reid on Religion," *Journal of Scottish Philosophy*, 19(3), pp. 261–274.

Callergård, Robert (2010) "Thomas Reid's Newtonian Theism: His Differences with the Classical Arguments of Richard Bentley and William Whiston," *Studies in History and Philosophy of Science*, 41, pp. 109–118.

Calvin, John (1960) *Institutes of the Christian Religion* (2 Vol). Edited by John T. McNeil. Translated by Ford L. Battles. Philadelphia, PA: The Westminster Press (Library of Christian Classics, XX).

Copenhaver, Rebecca (2015) "Thomas Reid on Aesthetic Perception," in Rebecca Copenhaver and Todd Buras (eds.) *Thomas Reid on Mind, Knowledge, and Value*. Oxford: Oxford University Press (Mind Association Occasional Series), pp. 124–138.

Copenhaver, Rebecca and Buras, Todd (eds.) (2015) *Thomas Reid on Mind, Knowledge, and Value*. Oxford: Oxford University Press (Mind Association Occasional Series).

Cuneo, Terence (2020) *Thomas Reid on the Ethical Life*. Cambridge: Cambridge University Press (Cambridge Elements in Ethics).

Daniels, Norman (1974) *Thomas Reid's Inquiry: The Geometry of Visibles and the Case for Realism*. New York: B. Franklin.

Daniels, Norman (1989) *Thomas Reid's Inquiry: The Geometry of Visibles and the Case for Realism*. Stanford: Stanford University Press.

Davenport, Allan Wade (1987) "Reid's Indebtedness to Bacon," *The Monist*, 70(4), pp. 496–507.

Davis, William C. (2006) *Thomas Reid's Ethics: Moral Epistemology on Legal Foundations*. New York: Continuum (Continuum Studies in British Philosophy).

Descartes, René (1993) *Meditations on First Philosophy*. Third. Translated by D. A. Cress. Cambridge: Hackett.

Di Ceglie, Roberto (2020) "Thomas Reid: Philosophy, Science, and the Christian Revelation," *Journal of Scottish Philosophy*, 18(1), pp. 17–38.

Faurot, J. H. (1952) "The Development of Reid's Theory of Knowledge," *University of Toronto Quarterly*, 21(3), pp. 224–231.

Foster, James J. S. (2017) *Thomas Reid on Religion*. Exeter: Imprint Academic (Library of Scottish Philosophy).

Foster, James J. S. (2024) *Thomas Reid and the Defence of Duty*. Edinburgh: Edinburgh University Press (Edinburgh Studies in Scottish Philosophy).

Fraser, Alexander Campbell (1898) *Thomas Reid*. Edinburgh: Oliphant Anderson (Famous Scots). https://archive.org/details/thomasreid00frasuoft.

Greco, John (2004) "Reid's Reply to the Skeptic," in Terence Cuneo and René van Woudenberg (eds.) *The Cambridge Companion to Thomas Reid*. Cambridge: Cambridge University Press (Cambridge Companions to Philosophy). pp. 134–155

Harris, James A. (2010) "Reid on Hume on Justice," in S. Roeser (ed.) *Reid on Ethics*. London: Palgrave MacMillan (Philosophers in Depth), pp. 204–222.

Hume, David (1978) *A Treatise of Human Nature*. 2nd ed. Edited by Lewis A. Selby-Bigge and Peter H. Nidditch. Oxford: Clarendon Press.

Hume, David. (1997) *Enquiries Concerning Human Understanding and Concerning the Principles of Morals*. Edited by Lewis A. Selby-Bigge and Peter H. Nidditch. 3rd ed. Oxford: Clarendon Press.

Hume, David (1998) *Principal Writings on Religion including Dialogues Concerning Natural Religion and the Natural History of Religion*. Edited by John C. A. Gaskin. Oxford: Oxford University Press (Oxford World's Classics).

Jaffro, Laurent (2015) "Reid on Aesthetic Response and the Perception of Beauty," in Rebecca Copenhaver and Todd Buras (eds.) *Thomas Reid on Mind, Knowledge, and Value*. Oxford: Oxford University Press (Mind Association Occasional Series), pp. 161–177.

Kroeker, Esther (2011) "Reid's Moral Psychology: Animal Motives as Guides to Virtue," *Canadian Journal of Philosophy*, 41(S1: New Essays on Reid), pp. 122–141.

Kroeker, Esther (2024) "Perceiving Design? Reid's Design Discourse," *Journal of the History of Philosophy*, 62(2), pp. 239–262.

Mackinlay Jr., James (1843) "Memoir of the Rev. James Mackinlay, D. D.," in *James Mackinlay, Select Sermons. With a Memoir by His Son; and Published under His Superintendence*. Kilmarnock, Glasgow and Edinburgh, pp. 9–63.

Mackintosh, James (1846) "Dissertation on the Progress of History," in Robert J. Mackintosh (ed.) *The Miscellaneous Works of the Right Honorable Sir*

James Mackintosh: Three Volumes Complete in One. Philadelphia, PA: Carey & Hart, pp. 94–197.

Newton, Isaac (2016) *The Principia: The Authoritative Translation and Guide: Mathematical Principles of Natural Philosophy*. Translated by I. Bernard Cohen, Anne Whitman, and Julia Budenz. Berkeley, CA: University of California Press.

Nichols, Ryan and Yaffe, Gideon (2023) "Thomas Reid," *Stanford Encyclopedia of Philosophy*. https://plato.stanford.edu/archives/sum2023/entries/reid/.

Paley, William (1802) *Natural Theology: Or, Evidences of the Existence and Attributes of the Deity, Collected from the Appearances of Nature*. Philadelphia, PA: John Morgan.

Plantinga, Alvin (1983) "Reason and Belief in God," in Alvin Plantinga and Nicholas Wolterstorff (eds.) *Faith and Rationality: Reason and Belief in God*. Notre Dame, IN: University of Notre Dame Press, pp. 16–93.

Poore, Gregory S. (2015) "Theism, Coherence, and Justification in Thomas Reid's Epistemology," in Rebecca Copenhaver and Todd Buras (eds.) *Thomas Reid on Mind, Knowledge, and Value*. Oxford: Oxford University Press (Mind Association Occasional Series), pp. 213–231.

Popkin, Richard H. (1980) *The High Road to Pyrrhonism*. Edited by Richard A. Watson and James E. Force. Indianapolis, IN: Hackett.

Reid, Thomas (1990) *Practical Ethics: Being Lectures and Papers on Natural Religion, Self-Government, Natural Jurisprudence, and the Law of Nations*. Edited by Knud Haakonssen. Princeton, NJ: Princeton University Press.

Reid, Thomas (1995) *Thomas Reid on Animate Creation*. Edited by Paul B. Wood. Edinburgh: Edinburgh University Press (The Edinburgh Edition of Thomas Reid, 1).

Reid, Thomas (2002a) *Essays on the Intellectual Powers of Man*. Edited by Derek R. Brookes. Edinburgh: Edinburgh University Press (The Edinburgh Edition of Thomas Reid, 3).

Reid, Thomas (2002b) *The Correspondence of Thomas Reid*. Edited by Paul B. Wood. Edinburgh: Edinburgh University Press (The Edinburgh Edition of Thomas Reid, 4).

Reid, Thomas (2003) *An Inquiry into the Human Mind on the Principles of Common Sense*. Second. Edited by Derek R. Brookes. Edinburgh: Edinburgh University Press (The Edinburgh Edition of Thomas Reid, 2).

Reid, Thomas (2004) *Thomas Reid on Logic, Rhetoric and Fine Arts*. Edited by Alexander Broadie. Edinburgh: Edinburgh University Press (The Edinburgh Edition of Thomas Reid, 5).

Reid, Thomas (2007) *Thomas Reid on Practical Ethics*. Edited by Knud Haakonssen. Edinburgh: Edinburgh University Press (The Edinburgh Edition of Thomas Reid, 6).

Reid, Thomas (2010) *Essays on the Active Powers of Man*. Edited by Knud Haakonssen and J. A. Harris. Edinburgh: Edinburgh University Press (The Edinburgh Edition of Thomas Reid, 7).

Reid, Thomas (2017) *Thomas Reid on Mathematics and Natural Philosophy*. Edited by Paul B. Wood. Edinburgh: Edinburgh University Press (Edinburgh Edition of Thomas Reid, 9).

Reid, Thomas (2021) *Thomas Reid and the University*. Edited by Paul B. Wood. Edinburgh: Edinburgh University Press (The Edinburgh Edition of Thomas Reid, 10).

Roeser, Sabine (ed.) (2010) *Reid on Ethics*. New York: Palgrave Macmillan (Philosophers in depth).

Rowe, William L. (1991) *Thomas Reid on Freedom and Morality*. Ithaca: Cornell University Press.

Rysiew, Patrick (2002) "Reid and Epistemic Naturalism," *The Philosophical Quarterly*, 52(209), pp. 437–456.

Sextus Empiricus (2000) *Outlines of Scepticism*. Translated by Julia Annas and Jonathan Barnes. Cambridge: Cambridge University Press (Cambridge Texts in the History of Philosophy).

Sher, Richard (2015) *Church and University in the Scottish Enlightenment: The Moderate Literati of Edinburgh*. 2nd ed. Edinburgh: Edinburgh University Press (Edinburgh Classic Editions).

Shrock, Christopher A. (2017) *Thomas Reid and the Problem of Secondary Qualities*. Edinburgh: Edinburgh University Press (Edinburgh Studies in Scottish Philosophy).

Somerville, James (1995) *The Enigmatic Parting Shot*. Aldershot: Avebury Press.

Sosa, Ernest (2009) *Reflective Knowledge: Apt Belief and Reflective Knowledge, Vol. II*. Oxford: Clarendon Press.

Stephen, Sir Leslie (1902) *History of English Thought in the Eighteenth Century*. 3rd ed. London: John Murray.

Stewart, M. Alexander (2004) "Rational Religion and Common Sense," in J. Houston (ed.) *Thomas Reid: Context, Influence, Significance*. Edinburgh: Dunedin Academic Press, pp. 123–160.

Tuggy, Dale (2004) "Reid's Philosophy of Religion," in Terence Cuneo and René van Woudenberg (eds.) *The Cambridge Companion to Thomas Reid*. Cambridge: Cambridge University Press (Cambridge Companions to Philosophy), pp. 289–312.

Van Cleve, James (2015) *Problems from Reid*. New York: Oxford University Press.

Wolterstorff, Nicholas (2001) *Thomas Reid and the Story of Epistemology.* Cambridge: Cambridge University Press (Modern European Philosophy).

Wolterstorff, Nicholas (2004) "God and Darkness in Reid," in Joseph Houston (ed.) *Thomas Reid: Context, Influence, Significance.* Edinburgh: Dunedin Academic Press, pp. 77–102.

Wood, Paul (forthcoming) *The Life of Thomas Reid*. Edinburgh: Edinburgh University Press.

Zuckert, Rachel (2015) "Thomas Reid's Expressivist Ethics," in Rebecca Copenhaver and Todd Buras (eds.) *Thomas Reid on Mind, Knowledge, and Value*. Oxford: Oxford University Press (Mind Association Occasional Series), pp. 139–160.

For Gordon Graham,
who first introduced me to Reid

Cambridge Elements ⹀

The Problems of God

Series Editor

Michael L. Peterson
Asbury Theological Seminary

Michael L. Peterson is Professor of Philosophy at Asbury Theological Seminary. He is the author of *God and Evil* (Routledge); *Monotheism, Suffering, and Evil* (Cambridge University Press); *With All Your Mind* (University of Notre Dame Press); *C. S. Lewis and the Christian Worldview* (Oxford University Press); *Evil and the Christian God* (Baker Book House); and *Philosophy of Education: Issues and Options* (Intervarsity Press). He is co-author of *Reason and Religious Belief* (Oxford University Press); *Science, Evolution, and Religion: A Debate about Atheism and Theism* (Oxford University Press); and *Biology, Religion, and Philosophy* (Cambridge University Press). He is editor of *The Problem of Evil: Selected Readings* (University of Notre Dame Press). He is co-editor of *Philosophy of Religion: Selected Readings* (Oxford University Press) and *Contemporary Debates in Philosophy of Religion* (Wiley-Blackwell). He served as General Editor of the Blackwell monograph series Exploring Philosophy of Religion and is founding Managing Editor of the journal *Faith and Philosophy*.

About the Series

This series explores problems related to God, such as the human quest for God or gods, contemplation of God, and critique and rejection of God. Concise, authoritative volumes in this series will reflect the methods of a variety of disciplines, including philosophy of religion, theology, religious studies, and sociology.

Cambridge Elements ☰

The Problems of God

Elements in the Series

A full series listing is available at: www.cambridge.org/EPOG

Printed in the United States
by Baker & Taylor Publisher Services